Bernard O'Leary,
Sacred Heart, Westminster

THE COUNCIL AND REUNION

HANS KÜNG

Professor in the Catholic Theology Faculty
of the University of Tübingen

THE COUNCIL AND REUNION

translated by
CECILY HASTINGS

SHEED AND WARD
LONDON AND NEW YORK

FIRST PUBLISHED 1961
SECOND IMPRESSION 1962
SHEED AND WARD, LTD
33 MAIDEN LANE
LONDON W.C.2
AND
SHEED AND WARD, INC
64 UNIVERSITY PLACE
NEW YORK 3

Originally published as
Konzil und Wiedervereinigung, 3rd ed., 1961
by Verlag Herder, Freiburg im Breisgau,
Germany

IMPRIMI PROTEST
ROTTENBURGI.   DIE 19 APRILIS, 1961
VICARIUS GENERALIS DR. KNAUPP

This book is set in 11 on 12 pt. Linotype Baskerville

Made and printed in Great Britain by
William Clowes and Sons, Limited, London and Beccles

INTRODUCTORY MESSAGE TO THE GERMAN EDITION

It is a happy omen to find a theologian responding to the stimulus provided by the Holy Father when he announced the holding of an Ecumenical Council; to see, with his help, in all loyalty to the Church, the perspectives that are opening before us concerning the divisions in Christendom and the hopes offered by the coming Council. I hope that this book, and the challenge which it presents, will be received with understanding, and spread far and wide.

FRANCIS, CARDINAL KÖNIG
ARCHBISHOP OF VIENNA

INTRODUCTORY MESSAGE TO THE FRENCH EDITION

We owe our gratitude to Editions du Cerf for making available to the French public, in the excellent translation of the Benedictine Fathers of Ligugé, the work published in German by Hans Küng, Professor in the Faculty of Catholic Theology at the University of Tübingen, under the title *The Council and Reunion*.

There are many Christians of all communions who long for that unity which Jesus Christ willed, and who place in the coming Council their hopes that a way may be opened to it. They will be happy to find out from this book how the Catholic Church, as she works for her own renewal throughout, can make a useful contribution to helping on the return to unity, in a common adherence to "the truth which makes free".

✠ ACHILLE CARDINAL LIENART
BISHOP OF LILLE
Superior of the Mission de France

". . . 'fiet unum ovile et unus pastor' (Jo. 10.16).
Quae quidem suavissima spes iam Nos duxit
vehementerque excitavit ad propositum illud
publice enuntiandum, Oecumenicum videlicet
cogendi Concilium, ad quod sacrorum Antistites,
de gravibus religionis rebus tractaturi, ex uni-
verso terrarum orbe convenient, ea praesertim
de causa, ut ad Catholicae Fidei incrementum
et ad rectam christiani populi morum renova-
tionem deveniatur, utque ecclesiastica disciplina
ad nostrorum temporum necessitates rationesque
aptius accommodetur. Id profecto mirabile prae-
bebit veritatis, unitatis, caritatisque spectaculum; spectaculum dicimus, quod ii etiam cer-
nentes, qui ab Apostolica hac Sede seiuncti sunt,
suave, ut confidimus, invitamentum accipient
ad illam unitatem quaerendam assequen-
damque, quam Jesus Christus a caelesti Patre
flagrantibus rogavit precibus."

". . . 'there will be one fold and one shepherd.'
(John 10.16.) This irresistible assurance was the
compelling motive which led Us to announce
publicly Our resolve to call an Ecumenical
Council. Bishops will come together there from
every corner of the world to discuss important

matters of religion. But the most pressing topics will be those which concern the spread of the Catholic faith, the revival of Christian standards of morality, and the bringing of ecclesiastical discipline into closer accord with the needs and conditions of our times. This in itself will provide an outstanding example of truth, unity and love. May those who are separated from this Apostolic See, beholding this manifestation of unity, derive from it the inspiration to seek out that unity which Jesus Christ prayed for so ardently from his heavenly Father."

Encyclical *Ad Petri Cathedram* of 29 June 1959
(translated as *Truth, Unity and Peace*,
London, C.T.S., 1959)

CONTENTS

xi

1. THE ECUMENICAL TASK OF THE CHURCH

JOHN XXIII's announcement of an Ecumenical Council was received with joy and in many quarters with enthusiasm; sometimes, admittedly, misdirected enthusiasm. The Pope's decision is epoch-making. Its first and very precious result has been a definite *change of atmosphere* both inside and outside the Church.

Inside the Catholic Church: Almost overnight the reunion of our separated brethren has ceased to be the concern only of a brave little vanguard, themselves objects of admiration, ridicule, pity or hostility; it has become the concern of the universal Church, even in purely Catholic countries, and of the Church's leaders; something to be not only proposed in theory but worked out in practice. Theological and pastoral work with an ecumenical slant are no longer regarded as hobbies for individuals but as a necessity for the entire Church. Within the Church today there is a longing and striving and praying for reunion of a totally new power and intensity. "Having before our eyes the most glowing pages of history that the centuries have to offer, we can be sure that the Ecumenical Council has already awakened in the hearts of

our bishops and priests a firm intention and a
more urgent desire to extend the frontiers of
Christian love, and to take their stand on their
own ground with their thoughts clear and their
hearts ready." (John XXIII, letter of 24 April
1959 to the Venetian clergy.)

Outside the Catholic Church: Despite some
exaggerated hopes at the beginning, the non-
Catholic communions forming the World Council of Churches now realize and recognize with
joy that for the first time since the Reformation
the Catholic Church has abandoned her passive,
waiting attitude of detachment, delimitation
and periodic appeals to return to the Church;
that through the personal initiative of her chief
shepherd she is now coming out to meet them,
vigorously and actively. Hopes for reunion have
risen by leaps and bounds since that announcement with its bold and sweeping vision—an
announcement which many prudent theologians
would doubtless have advised against, but which
the Pope decided upon with positively charismatic assurance. He himself writes, in the letter
quoted above, of "the Ecumenical Council,
which we announced in obedience to an inspiration felt in the humility of our heart as a sudden,
unexpected, direct touch". The Pope's courageous act has given an answer to men's longing
for unity, a longing which has often lain hidden
and which has been almost suffocated under

centuries of religious prejudice and political cross-purposes, of pettiness and spitefulness and downright slander and calumny. World reaction to the Pope's announcement was a proof of how much men of goodwill everywhere today are longing for this unity; and, it is equally necessary to say, how tired they are of having nothing to console them but such theological definitions and distinctions as are often hardly intelligible to anyone today.

Hopes for the Council, then, are great; but its possibilities are limited and must be assessed with extreme cool-headedness. An illusory enthusiasm for reunion can only do damage and deflect our energies from the enormous efforts which reunion in fact demands. One would have gathered, from several of the early reactions to the announcement of the Council, that it was enough just to sit down and talk round a table for a "reunion council" (cf. Lyons, 1274 or Florence, 1439) to take shape and a "reunion formula" to be worked out. Many Catholics, too, thought of it as a simple matter of a "return" of their separated brethren to the Catholic Church. All this is, of course, an illusion. It was not for nothing that the Pope himself, when he announced the Council, spoke of "carrying out a *threefold* plan", envisaging, along with the Council, the reform of canon law and a diocesan synod at Rome aimed at practical reform.

The third item in this programme was carried out in January 1960. Obviously, we cannot regard the Roman Synod as in every respect a model for the Ecumenical Council. A diocesan synod is concerned with the state of one diocese, an Ecumenical Council with the universal Church. A diocesan synod is subordinate to canon law and has only very limited powers for reform. An Ecumenical Council is above canon law; in union with the Pope it has universal legislative authority in every field of ecclesiastical law, and can thus carry out full-scale reform throughout the entire Church.

John XXIII's inaugural encyclical, quoted at the beginning of this book, has made it abundantly clear that the *suavissima spes* for reunion is bound up with the increase of the Catholic faith (*catholicae fidei incrementum*), with a true renewal of morality among Christian people ("recta christiani populi morum renovatio") and with the adaptation of ecclesiastical discipline to the needs and conditions of our time ("utque ecclesiastica disciplina ad nostrorum temporum necessitates rationesque aptius accommodetur"). This is what the Council is to do: something totally different from all the wholly theoretical and ineffectual appeals to "return" which have rung out so often. The Pope is confident that a Council which achieves these practical tasks will, as he says, itself be a gentle invitation ("suave, ut confidimus, invitamentum") to our separated brethren to seek and find true unity.

Summing up: The reunion of separated Christians, as conceived by John XXIII, is bound up with a renewal within the Catholic Church to which the coming Council is to make an essential contribution.

This view of the Council was brought out clearly by the Pope at an audience with the Oriental College. The Holy Father intimated that from the time when the idea came to him he had always had it in mind that this assembly would be concerned exclusively with the Catholic Church. She must adapt herself (the idea is better expressed by the Italian word *aggiornamento*); so much has changed in the modern world, both among the faithful themselves and in the way in which they have to live. This was the point which the Holy Father particularly made on January 25th. Hence the Church must work at this adaptation. When it has been done, then she can turn to her separated brethren and say: "See, this is what the Church is, what she does, what she looks like." Only when she appears thus healthily modernized and rejuvenated can she say to these separated brethren "Come to us." Today, clearly, it would be impossible and futile to embark upon endless discussions which would lead nowhere.

The Pope expressed himself particularly clearly (see the *Osservatore Romano*) in his address to the diocesan presidents of Italian Catholic Action: "The Ecumenical Council will be a demonstration, uniquely far-reaching in its significance, of truly world-wide catholicity. What is happening is proof that the Lord is assisting this salutary plan with his holy grace. The idea of the Council did not come as the slowly ripening fruit of long deliberation but was like the sudden flowering of an unexpected spring . . . By God's grace, then, we shall hold this Council; we shall prepare for it by working hard at whatever on the Catholic side most needs to be healed and strengthened according to the teaching of our Lord. When we have carried out this strenuous task, eliminated everything which could at the human level hinder our rapid progress, then we shall point to the Church in all her splendour, *sina macula et ruga*, and say to all those who are separated from us, Orthodox, Protestants, and the rest: Look, brothers, this is the Church of Christ. We have striven to be true to her, to ask the Lord for grace that she may remain forever what he willed. Come; here the way lies open for meeting and for homecoming; come; take, or resume, that place which is yours, which for many of you was your fathers' place. O what joy, what a flowering even in civil and social life, may be looked for by the whole world if we once have religious peace and the re-establishment of the family of Christendom!"[1]

Within this framework, the question of inviting non-Catholic Christians is a secondary one. The ambiguity in the meaning of the words "ecumenical" and "council" raised some false hopes here. In English, "council" has both the narrower sense of a council of the Church in its traditional meaning and the wider one of a parliament or assembly, as in the World Council of Churches. "Ecumenical", when used in connection with the latter, means interdenominational; whereas in its ancient traditional sense in Catholic canon law it means the assembly of all the Catholic bishops in so far as they are not prevented by external circumstances from attending. But according to the Pope's intention even a purely Roman Catholic Council, restricted to the Catholic *oikoumene*, will be ecumenical in the other sense of being the concern of all Christians. Not only because any council of the ancient Church is bound to be watched by all Christians with deep interest and real sympathy, not only because any Catholic council is bound to have important effects on interconfessional matters, but also and above all because this council, as the Pope intends it, is

[1] *Herder-Korrespondenz*, vol. 14 (1959–60), pp. 8 f.

meant to create the prerequisites for reunion. This leaves open the possibility of participation by non-Catholic theologians in preparatory meetings before the Council, and also of invitations to non-Catholic observers, with whom discussions could be held in special separate committees.[1] In any case, it seems that indirect non-Catholic co-operation (including help from the World Council of Churches) would be more fruitful in our present situation than direct participation in the Council, which would still, today, be premature.

As Professor E. Stakemeier, the well-known expert on the Council of Trent and on current Catholic-Protestant controversial writing, rightly observes:

> The "invitation to separated communions to seek for unity" is just as real if the Council creates a situation which will make it easier for those of the separated brethren who are seeking unity to be reunited with the Catholic Church. The Council could very well lay a foundation for fruitful interconfessional theological discussions, and could create such favourable conditions for reunion conversations as would bring about a *rapprochement*; of this there are already many hopeful signs.

[1] Cf. the Press conference given by Cardinal Tardini, the Cardinal Secretary of State (*Osservatore Romano*, 1 Nov. 1959).

In this connection Stakemeier quotes the Lutheran Superintendent Hugo Schnell:

> It was never our opinion that questions about who would be invited, how far afield the invitations would go, and what would be the status of those invited, were crucial questions. They are important, no doubt, but secondary. We should do well to realize that there are greater possibilities in discussion than in official participation . . . Since if non-Roman Churches did take part in the Council they would in any case be in the minority, their status in it would be irrelevant. There might be circumstances, when it came to voting, in which it would be preferable to take part as an observer rather than to have a vote.[1]

The direct task of the Council, then, is a renewal within the Church, or (as we can equally well say, with a precise nuance to which we shall return later) a reform within the Church. It will demonstrate before the very eyes of Christians both in and outside of the Church something which has always *in principle* been a commonplace of Catholicism: that reformation is not a Protestant preserve. All too often Protestant preachers and theologians in Europe and

[1] See E. Stakemeier, "Das kommende Konzil und die Einheit der Christen", in *Lebendiges Zeugnis*, June 1959, 6.

in the missions have used as a decisive weapon in argument the claim that they are the reformed Church, Catholics the unreformed Church. All too often, too, Catholic preachers and theologians have treated reform of the Church as practically and theologically tabu, as though the promises made to her excluded reform. True, the word "reform" has historical overtones on account of the Reformers' Reformation, known simply as such; moreover the Latin languages, in general, cannot, like the Germanic ones, make a distinction between reform in the general sense and Reformation in the Protestant sense; only in writing can capital letters overcome the ambiguity of *reformatio, la riforma, la réforme, la reforma*. But there is nothing radically sectarian about the word "reformed". True, "réformer" and "réformation" were among Calvin's favourite words. But as late as the Formula Concordiae the Lutheran Churches appear as "our Reformed Churches", while the Calvinists, on the other hand, go on describing themselves as "catholic". It is only in the last quarter of the sixteenth century that the Churches of the Formula Concordiae develop a preference for calling themselves "Lutheran", while the other Churches stemming from the Reformation call themselves "reformed", as an expression of their claim that it is only they who have taken the Reformation to its ultimate, radical goal. It is hence quite possible that the slogan *ecclesia semper refor-manda*, whose history has yet to be written, may have originated, perhaps quite recently, in Cal-vinistic circles.

But all this does not alter the fact that *re-formare*, meaning "to give another form", "to restore an earlier, better form", "to form anew something that has been deformed", "to shape something according to its own essential being", can be taken in a good sense and one which is firmly grounded in Catholic tradition. We find it already in the Vulgate: "Jesum Christum, qui reformabit corpus humilitatis nostrae"—"Jesus Christ, who will reform the body of our low-ness" (Phil. 3.21), and "Reformamini in novitate sensus vestri"—"Be reformed in the newness of your mind." (Rom. 12.2.) Hence we find the words *reformator* (used especially of Christ) and *reformare* (especially in the sense of *intus refor-mari*, "to be reformed within") used countless times in the liturgy, the Fathers and the medi-eval theologians.[1] After Constantine, when worldliness began to grow in the Church, they began to be used more and more with reference to the Church herself, precisely in the sense of Church reform, so that "reform of the Church in head and members" can be called the very

[1] For examples see the references given in Yves Congar, O.P., *Vraie et fausse réforme dans l'Eglise*, Paris, 1950, pp. 356 f.

watchword of the later Middle Ages. How much
was written on this theme at the time of the
Council of Constance! Nor must it be forgotten
that not only was *reformatio morum* one of the
subjects for discussion at the Ecumenical Council of Vienne (1311–12) but that as early as 1215,
when the great Pope Innocent III summoned
the Fourth Council of the Lateran, it was done
"propter reformationem universalis Ecclesiae",
"for the reformation of the whole Church", as
the Pope declared both in his proclamation of
the Council and in his opening address to it.[1]

Reformare, then, is a word with a solid foundation in Catholic tradition. Neither in theory
nor in practice has the necessity of reform in the
Catholic Church ever been disputed; neither in
the high Middle Ages, nor in the age of the
Renaissance and Reformation, nor, obviously,
in the reforming period of Trent and after
Trent. So we can speak equally well either of
renewal or of reform of the Church. What
matters primarily is not which word we prefer
but how we interpret it. What matters is, (1),
the theological basis we give to a renewal or
reform of the Church, (2), our basic theological
understanding of its nature, possibilities and
limitations, and (3), how it is put into practice,
in past history and at the present day. A fundamental theological and historical consideration

[1] *Patrologia Latina,* 216, 824 and 217, 673.

of the question is a necessity before a council; it is of particular urgency before this council, with its special internal and interdenominational problems. So we will now discuss, if only briefly and cursorily:

(1) The permanent necessity of renewal in the Church.

(2) The manner and mode of Catholic renewal.

(3) What Catholic renewal has in practice been in the past and is in the present.

From a combination of these points we shall get some light on the concrete tasks with which the proposed Ecumenical Council is faced.

2. THE PERMANENT NECESSITY OF RENEWAL IN THE CHURCH

IN ordinary daily life we are always hearing the Church being spoken of in two different ways. The "idealist", clerical or lay, whether preaching, giving instruction, or in ordinary conversation, sees the Church as the Church of God; pure, spotless, blameless, holy, concerned only with the salvation of men and the glory of God. The "realist", the man in the street or the bar or reading his paper, sees the Church as a Church of men; all too human, both in head and members; a harsh, intolerant machine, opposed to freedom and greedy for power, immersed in the finance and politics of this world, full of every kind of failing. Who is right? Both are, in different ways—and both are wrong. Right, in so far as the Church in a sense *is* what each of them sees (though "is" has to be understood analogically); wrong in so far as they see the Church *only* thus, exclusively and onesidedly. Both idealist and realist are fundamentally uninterested in a renewal of the Church. The idealist, seeing only the light side of the Church, thinks it unnecessary; the realist, limited to the dark side, thinks it impossible. Only those who, genuinely caring about the Church whose members they are, dare to see the darkness and still believe in the light can be open and ready for a renewal of the Church such as the Pope expects from the Council. So do not be alarmed if in this chapter we look hard at the darkness in the Church. Such a view *is* onesided. But it is not an end in itself and does not describe the whole or even the essential.

By the Church we understand "the People of God of the New Testament, founded by Jesus Christ, hierarchically organized, serving to advance the reign of God and the salvation of men; and which exists as the mystical body of Christ".[1] In a comprehensive definition of the Church there is no real opposition between the two views customarily stressed in Catholic and Protestant theology respectively: the Church seen (by Catholics) as coming from God, "ecclesia in Spiritu Sancto adunata", united in the Holy Spirit, and the Church seen (by Protestants) as springing from men, as the *congregatio fidelium,* the congregation of the faithful. Even the Roman Catechism, in its definition of the Church, gives the Greco-Latin word *ecclesia* (from *ekkaleo,* call forth) the meaning of "assembly" ("and she is rightly called Ecclesia, because she summons and assembles all for salvation"); and it describes the Church as follows:

[1] Schmaus, *Katholische Dogmatik,* Munich, 1958, vol. 3, pp. 1, 48.

"According to the common usage of Holy Writ, this word is used . . . for the Christian community, and only for the assemblies of the faithful (*fidelium congregationes*); i.e., for those who have been called to the light of the truth and knowledge of God by faith, so that they may put away the darkness of ignorance and error, in piety and holiness adore the true and living God, and serve him with their whole heart. To express all this in a word, the Church is, as St. Augustine says, the faithful people spread over all the earth".[1] The Church is indeed essentially a creation of God through Jesus Christ in his Holy Spirit; her being can be conceived only in faith, as a holy mystery from above. But the Church must not be seen only from above; she must not be deified, as though she did not consist of real men, of men as they really are. In her very foundation the two sides were there: the call of Christ her founder, and the obedient response of weak human beings. It is only in terms of Jesus Christ that the Church can rightly be understood; she is his body, his earthly manifestation, and in her as in him the divine and the human are permanently bound together. Until the end of time the Church will remain at once a divine mystery and a human structure;

[1] *Catechismus ex Decreto Ss. Concilii Tridentini ad Parochos Pii V. Pont. Max. Jussu Editus.*, ed. Bassani, 1833, pp. 65–6.

one single mystery of light and shadow. This is the only thing that makes sense of a renewal and reform of the Church. And we now have to make this clearer at two levels, which in practice interpenetrate. Renewal and reform of the Church are permanently necessary because the Church consists, first, of human beings, and, secondly, of sinful human beings.

1. THE CHURCH IS MADE OF HUMAN BEINGS

The world is never what it ought to be. Where there are men there is always failure, and where there is failure, there is need for improvement. What is deformed must be reformed. Hence, in the secular sphere, reform, and the constant introduction of new reforms, are simply taken for granted, not only by the crusading fanatic but equally by the man in the street, who spontaneously raises his voice in opposition to any bad state of affairs and demands that it be put right.

This is so in the world. But the Church is, precisely, *not* the world, understanding "the world" at this stage simply in its ordinary, human, visible sense. In the ultimate ground of her being, the life of the Holy Spirit of Jesus Christ, the Church is actually invisible, or, we might also say, visible only to the believer. She

lives wholly by the grace of God, she is God's
spiritual temple, the mysterious reality of the
body of Jesus Christ. The power that gives her
her form and structure is his Holy Spirit. It is
he, the invisible, who founds the Church each
day anew, who awakens and animates and en-
lightens her, makes her active and effective. It is
he who causes her to lead her spiritual life as
the community of grace and faith and love.
What is there here for human beings to reform?

The Church is not the world, the Church is
not of this world, but *the Church is in this
world*. Precisely as the *people* of God, precisely
as the *body* of Christ, the Church, for all her
invisibility, is at the same time visible in the
human beings and the organization which form
her; she can be perceived historically, psycho-
logically, sociologically. The Church is an institution set up by God through Christ which, as a
community of believers always animated, moved
and formed afresh by the Holy Spirit, is forever
coming into being anew in the activity of her
members. She has the character both of personal
event and of institutional existence. By analogy
with the God-Man, whose body she is, the
Church is both visible and invisible; visible in
the preaching of the word, for which Christ set
up the apostolic office, in the celebration of the
sacraments, in the confession of faith and the

practice of love. From the very time of her foundation the Church was a definite, delimited, organized community, with men in charge of her, with rules, rites and customs; and so today she remains visible in her individual members, in her preaching of the word, in her administration of the sacraments and in her law. As the Church of God made of men and for men, as a divine-*human* mystery, she is set in the dimensions of space and time; she is an earthly, historical fact, whose divine institutions and constitutions work themselves out on the human side in various intellectual, ritual, social, legal and aesthetic forms. Being in time, the Church can never be perfected on this earth. Time never stands still, and so the Church cannot but keep marching forward. In every age she is faced with the difficult task of presenting herself anew. God's Church, made of men, is in the world and in its history.

But this also means that the world and its history are in the Church. The most widely differing mentalities and cultures, languages and backgrounds, questions and answers have contributed to shaping the two-thousand-year-old face of the Church. Often, in setting their imprint upon her, they have brought a development and enrichment of the Church, but often too it has been a deformation and constriction.

Jesus Christ, her head, continues his own empty-
ing out of himself in his body which is the
Church:

Christ our Lord, in the mysterious process
of his Incarnation, accepted a tremendous
humiliation of himself, a *kenosis*: He, the Son
of God, entered into the limitations of
humanity, into the concrete finitude of his
own bodily structure, into the smallness and
narrowness of circumstances with all the limitations of space and time, and especially into
all the terrible reality of what human beings
could do, from the Manger to the Cross. In
the same way his body, the Church, as she
enters into the movement of history, necessarily undergoes an emptying-out, a humiliation of her true self; that is to say, she can
only indirectly and imperfectly, only in dis-
continuous flashes, reflect that mysterious
heavenly glory which is truly at the root of
her being.[1]

True, in what she is essentially—that is, in
what she has from Christ—the Church is in-
destructible. But the particular historical form
which God's Church takes in the world and its
history can only ever be a realization of one
among all the possible forms of the Church in

[1] Karl Adam, *Das Wesen des Katholizismus*, 11th ed.,
Düsseldorf, 1946, p. 248.

different ages; along with gain, this means that there is always loss or at least the danger of loss. Such instances as these have often been suggested:[1]

The Jewish world, with its unshakable monotheism, its messianic hope and its penetration of every aspect of life by religion, brought to the Church all that the Old Testament means to Christ and to Christians; but at the same time it brought a nationalistic narrowness and an externalized piety of good works and the Law.

The Greek world, with its secular wisdom, its sense of beauty and its deeply human quality, brought the Church a universal language and a profound intellectual interpretation of revelation, a magnificent synthesis of the Church's teaching expressed in new concepts and new uses of words, and a compelling statement of the glory of the Christian's privilege in being taken into the life of God; but it also brought a measure of intellectualist rationalization, of exaggerated speculation and sterilely conceptual mysticism, an over anthropocentric doctrine of grace and a dualism which made an enemy of matter and the body.

The Roman world, with its sense of form, law, organization, authority, tradition and unity,

[1] Cf. e.g., Karl Adam, "Das Problem des Geschichtlichen im Leben der Kirche", *Tübinger Theologische Quartalschrift*, 128 (1948), 257–300.

2 + C.A.R.

and for everything that is practical and useful, brought the Church something both necessary in itself and implied in her nature as a body: the working out of Church order and canon law, and the use of definite methods in the direction of affairs; but with this it brought power politics and authoritarian traditionalism, formalism and legalism both in theory and in practice.

The Germanic world, with its sense of freedom, imagination and subjectivity, brought the Church its own kind of religious art and a personal interiorization of religion; intense, personally experienced feeling and a healthy dissatisfaction with torpidity and externalization; but it also brought misty subjectivism and anarchical caprice, crude superstition, undisciplined mysticism and sectarianism.

Thus the necessary process by which the Church, for all her essential indestructibility, takes a particular shape in history implies not only a certain unavoidable limitation and one-sidedness, but, alas, beyond this, because of human weakness, a certain process of deformation as well: inadequacies and actual damage, fatal overstressing of what is right in itself to the obscuring of what is at least as important, misplacement of emphasis, excessive growth in some one direction, developing at last (if not openly, at least implicitly) to the point where it solidifies into heresy.

The process of formation and deformation has not been the same during the second thousand years as it was during the first. Despite the steady branching out of the Church, we can hardly avoid observing that there has been at the same time a progressive narrowing: even in the first millennium in regard to Judaism, then at the beginning of the second in regard to the Christian East, then to modern Europe, and finally to non-European cultures and religions. While the Church, like St. Paul, became Greek to the Greeks and barbarian to the barbarians, it has not been Arab to the Arabs, Negro to the Negroes, Indian to the Indians nor Chinese to the Chinese. The Church of Jesus Christ, taken as a whole, has remained a European-American affair. We might adduce several causes for this sad and disconcerting fact. But it cannot be disputed that much of the fault lies with an increasingly closed and fixed immobility in the Church (and in her missionary methods) which develops as time goes on. Indeed, it has been so in Europe too. Despite ever-increasing secularization, the Church has not been, during her second millennium, the intellectual *avant-garde,* as she was, on the whole, during her first thousand years. While the world has blithely developed on autonomous, non-religious lines and has

forged ever more swiftly ahead in its enthusiastic pursuit of progress, the Church has seemed
to lag more and more behind, identified more
and more with the *ancien régime* and reaction;
a seemingly inhospitable isolationist Church
(despite various concessions and adaptations), a
Church which has to a large extent lost the
world. The fault was certainly not the Church's
alone; nor—unless we are prepared to make the
Middle Ages into an absolute standard—can
we deny the right reason in the process by which
man's activities and organization at the natural
level have developed their autonomy; nor are
we denying the many positive aspects in the
Church in our own times. But we in the Church
today cannot shirk the question, humiliating
and painful as it is: Is it not the case that while
interest in religion in general is today on the
increase, adherence to the Church is still on the
decline? How many people today still believe
in the Church's message, how many actually
live the Faith, how many are there practising,
with any regularity or inner conviction? In
Paris, in Rome, in Berlin, in London or New
York, in all the countless cities of "Christian"
Europe and "Christian" America; or, indeed,
in their country districts either, now neo-pagan
or never (consider South America) thoroughly
Christianized? Are we to settle down with this
catastrophic falling-away from the Church as

though it were something to be accepted as unalterable, like the weather? We can understand how an alert and responsible shepherd of his flock like Cardinal Suhard could, in his anguish over the dechristianization of these millions, find courage and energy for bold countermeasures. We can understand how the Pope has called urgently for a better adaptation of the Church to the conditions of our times, for a modernization of her pastoral work.

But many devout Christians are too little worried by all this. They take too onesided a view of the ill-will in the world, and fail to take the Church's own faults seriously. What really exasperates the modern man (both outside and inside the Church), far more than the sins of her members, is the lack of any openness among the Church's leaders, at every level, towards new problems and insights, new forms and values; their narrowness, their procrastination—in short, the long series of historical mistakes, which are facts, though they are apt to be soft-pedalled inside the Church. Is the modern man completely wrong about this? God keep the Church from "modernity", and keep her different from the world! There are "adaptations" which would be mere surrender to fashion, and ultimately sheer betrayal of the ever-out-of-season Gospel of Jesus Christ. The Church is in her very essence bound to that Gospel and so to tradition. But we must ask ourselves here, is there not also a *refusal* to adapt which is just as much a sheer betrayal—a betrayal of Christ's missionary charge to the Apostles and of St. Paul's call to be "all things to all men"; a cowardly withdrawal from the present age into a spurious, self-righteous "splendid isolation"? It would not be honest to deny that it has happened often enough; we in the Church have failed to go half-way to meet men in situations where they had a right to expect it; we have bristled up defensively when we could have given cheerful approval; we have defended the good with evil weapons; we have defended the indefensible. We have invoked the authority of the Gospel in cases where nothing more was in fact involved than an established philosophy, mentality, culture or system, which we might have invoked or perhaps better not have invoked at all. We have condemned things that had later —when it was too late—to be admitted, and finally blessed and claimed as our own.

The Church has been blamed for all of this, and often too severely blamed. She has been blamed all the more because it is easy to get the impression that since the eleventh century, and even more since the thirteenth, she has tended to be aware of, and to stress before the world, not, as in patristic times, her existence as a heavenly mystery, but rather her earthly organization, the plenitude of her legal powers, the

lawfulness of her claims. Engaged in an un-
balanced apologetic stressing only her holiness
and infallibility, she would refuse to admit, in
all honesty and humility, that errors had
occurred even in cases where she was perfectly
capable of error and in simple fact had erred
(among many other instances, we are constantly
reminded of the case of Galileo and the whole
relationship of the Church to the natural
sciences, on the one hand, and the interpretation
of the Bible, on the other.)

It has often been very difficult to maintain
the tension which is characteristically Catholic
between authority and freedom. It has often
been hard to distinguish between the real
essence of a thing and some particular current
form of it, e.g., between some essential office or
authority and the unworthy exercise of it.
Failures in the exercise of ecclesiastical office
have indeed been one special form of the burden
under which the Church labours; and here again
it has often been a self-satisfied inability, de-
nounced by Christ himself, to read the "signs of
the times", a placid, neglectful inactivity where
there should have been well-planned, courageous
initiatives in the exercise of the pastoral, teaching and priestly office, which have proved a
heavier burden than the particular moral shortcomings of individuals. The temptations of Jesus

himself referred less to the individual than to his messianic office.[1]

Thus we have the world within the Church. We have to realize the immense difficulty of the Church's task in her journey down the ages if we are to avoid judging her harshly, self-righteously, and as though looking down from some superior plane. This Church, made as she is of men, *in* the world and yet not *of* the world, has no easy task in steering her course between Scylla and Charybdis, between surrender to the world on the left and hostility to the world on the right. It may be a help, and a help to those inside the Church who are often too little aware of her tremendous difficulties, if we give a brief outline here of certain types of danger to which the Church is subject, certain wrong developments and wrong attitudes which are possible within her.

On the left lies the threat of *surrender to the world*. The Church has to be *in* the world and *for* the world; but the very fact that she exists *for* the world has often, for the sake of the world's salvation, to take the form of being *against* the world. Her norm can never be the "elements" of the world and the law of the world, but only Jesus Christ. But the Church, being of men, is

[1] For the temptations of Jesus as temptations of the Church see P. Simon, *Das Menschliche in der Kirche Christi*, Freiburg im Breisgau, 1948, pp. 1–9.

forever under the temptation to make herself at
home in the world, to regard her worldly
successes as the coming of the Kingdom of God,
to be intent only on making herself secure and
powerful and free from opposition and persecution; to involve herself with some particular
economic or social system, with some form of
government or pattern of society or of thought,
with a nation or a class or a particular line in
politics: with some one fixed mental picture of
the world or of humanity. It is very easy for her
to develop fixed forms and find herself almost
inextricably entangled in them, to conquer the
world and be thereby conquered by the world.
From being bound to the world she then becomes conformed to it, adopting a worldly spirit
and making use of means, methods and institutions which are alien to the Gospel. From
addressing herself to the present time, she turns
to surrendering herself to it, through modernity
at any price and a merely external adaptation
to the external technical achievements of one
particular age. These are really serious dangers.
It would be possible for someone to identify
himself, externally, with the whole modern trend
of our times, and yet to have understood nothing
of the real *needs* of our time and of the *true*
adaptation of the Church to it. One could be
deeply in love with some modern, world-wide,
ecclesiastical form of the American Way of Life

2*

and yet not have the faintest understanding of the liturgical, biblical, theological, missionary, organizational and social renewal of the Church. The history of the Church bears testimony to the fact that the Church, being made of men, has been constantly threatened by this danger of Sadduceeism: conformism, opportunism, modernism.

To the left, then, the Church, becoming subject to the world, is in danger of becoming worldly; but to the right, becoming hostile to the world, she is in danger of becoming "churchy". The Church has to be in the world and for the world but not of the world; for Christ's own sake she has to remain, ultimately, alien to it, forever swimming against the stream. Yet she must not live for herself alone, leaving the world to be the world; she has to be the leaven in the world, intent upon the coming of the Kingdom of God. But the Church, being made of men, is forever under the temptation to make herself at home within her own walls: to become the goal instead of only the way, to regard her organization as an end in itself, and so to make the attainment of the true goal harder instead of more possible and easier. The Church, pursuing her difficult journey, is here beset by a multitude of extremely concrete dangers, and if we are to judge her situation rightly it is absolutely necessary to see perfectly clearly how it is precisely what is best that can be misused (remembering that *abusus non tollit usum*). The danger of becoming "churchy" can take innumerable forms. It is there when piety gives way to external Church practices; the care of souls to ecclesiastical administration; the Pope and bishops to bureaucracy; the missions to religious propaganda; the apostolate to a struggle for social position and spheres of influence; charismatic gifts to unimaginative, routine administration; spiritual leadership to petty paternalism; preaching to dry rationalism or false rhetoric; the Sermon on the Mount to spiritual juridicalism; ecclesiastical discipline to the legalism of the Talmud; the sacraments to commercialized rites; the liturgy to empty ceremonies; zeal for the Lord to "getting results"; spiritual growth to Church statistics; ancient tradition to established custom; the word of God to current ideas; the Gospel to a theological system; orthodoxy in doctrine to denunciation; unity to uniformity; faith in the Church to faith in a machine: in a word, when letter replaces spirit. Of course none of this *need* happen; but it *can* happen. There is always the danger that the spirit may become fossilized in permanent "ecclesiastical" forms, customs, regulations; that the life of the Body of Christ may become formalized and bureaucratized. A Church thus turned in upon herself would become, in her relations with the world, a polemically defensive ghetto-Church; clinging rigidly to forms whose value is all in the past, she would be unable even to hear the demand for new ones, and would hold aloof from the world in proud self-sufficiency. Such a Church would mirror only herself, praising herself instead of the Lord; her arrogant sense of superiority over against the world would be only the reverse side of a sense of inferiority. The root attitude in such a Church would be fear: fear of progress in the world and in history, fear of anything that had not already been tried, of the unaccustomed, the out-of-the-ordinary; fear of necessary changes, of risks, uncertainties, experiments, adventures. Here too ecclesiastical history bears testimony to the fact that the Church, being of men, has been constantly threatened by this danger, the danger of Pharisaism: confessionalism, immobility, traditionalism.

The Church gone worldly and the Church gone churchy, Sadduceeism and Pharisaism, are not fundamentally so very different. Each induces the other, so that a worldly Church would always be in some sense churchy as well, and vice versa. As enemies of Christ they are friends of one another. The fact that the Church has never gone under entirely to these enemies, never been simply as bad as the worst we have been describing, is precisely the miracle of Christ's Spirit in the Church. Thanks to this we can, with joy and satisfaction, take note of all the significant progress the Church has made in this century; the morale of Church and clergy has not always been as good as it is now. But let us not be too optimistic: it is another matter if we consider, for instance, the Church's effect upon the world and her spiritual presence in it. Does not the Church, in spite of her externally heightened prestige, often seem rather to be lingering on as a mere decoration for certain private and public occasions? How much does she really have to say, *spiritually,* in that central arena of modern life where the questions essential to present and future are decided? Has the Church not to a considerable extent lost her power to draw men to her, especially the workers and the leaders of intellectual life? And what significance does she have among the awakening peoples of Asia? It is impossible to ignore the fact that the Church has been to a great extent thrust out of modern life and history. With the present breaking down around us in unprecedented fashion, in the midst of a new age which has already begun, it is more urgent than ever that we should make a painfully critical, dispassionate analysis, the kind of description which will appear onesided, of the weaknesses in the Church's position. It is an indispensable condition of that renewal of the Church which the Pope expects.

2. THE CHURCH IS MADE OF SINNERS

We have spoken of the visible Church in the
world, meaning the world in its ordinary,
human, visible sense. But we must go deeper.
Ultimately it is a question not of the created
world but of the world of "the flesh"; not simply
of secular history but of sinful history; not only
of failure and deformation but of sin and vice;
not only of historical errors which do not lie
personally at anyone's door, but of personal guilt.

In this sense the world is the kingdom of evil,
of sin, of the devil. But the Church is not the
world. She is the body of Jesus Christ and his
spotless bride, purified, hallowed, enlivened by
the Spirit: the fullness of Christ. We acknowledge her precisely as set apart from the world,
the *holy* Church. Her Lord is he who alone is
holy, her head is the Holy One of God, her spirit
is the Holy Spirit, the word she proclaims is the
Holy Gospel, the power that works in her and
through her is the holy and hallowing power of
the sacraments, her people are the Holy People
of God. "Ecclesia sancta, ecclesia sanctorum":
the Church whose members are even now sancti-
fied in the Holy Spirit and so are even now holy.
What is there here for human beings to reform?

The Church is not the world, but here too we
must say that the Church is in the world—and

the world is in the Church. Cardinal Newman makes us penetratingly aware of it:

> Now, the true account of this is, that the Church so far from being literally, and in fact, separate from the wicked world, is within it. The Church is a body, gathered together in the world, and in a process of separation from it. The world's power, alas! is over the Church, because the Church has gone forth into the world to save the world. All Christians are in the world, and of the world, so far as sin has dominion over them; and not even the best of us is clean every whit from sin. Though then, in our idea of the two, and in their principles, and in their future prospects, the Church is one thing, and the world is another, yet in present matter of fact, the Church is of the world, not separate from it; for the grace of God has but partial possession even of religious men, and the best that can be said of us is, that we have two sides, a light side and a dark, and that the dark happens to be outermost. Thus we form part of the world to each other, though we be not of the world.[1]

All holiness during this earthly pilgrimage is precarious. The Church is the *communio sanctorum,* but, alas, the *communio peccatorum* too;

[1] J. H. Newman, *Parochial and Plain Sermons,* London, 1875, 7, 3, pp. 35-6.

the Epistles, and the Apocalypse even more, testify that this was so even in her glorious beginnings. She is the Church of poor sinners, who can and must pray every day afresh, "Forgive us our trespasses."

Still more palpable and painful does the conflict between the power of God and the weakness of man become when the in-streaming life of grace and truth is checked by human passions, by sin and vice, when Christ as He is realized in human history is dragged through the dust of the street, through the common-place and the trivial, and over masses of rubbish. That is the deepest tragedy, the very tragedy of the Divine, when It is dispensed by unworthy hands and received by unworthy lips. An immoral laity, bad priests, bishops and popes—these are the saddest wounds of the Body of the mystical Christ. This is what grieves the earnest Catholic and inspires his sorrowful lamentation, when he sees these wounds and is unable to help. "The Church," says Cardinal Newman, "is ever ailing, and lingers on in weakness, 'always bearing about in the body the dying of the Lord Jesus, that the life also of Jesus might be made manifest in her body'." It is an essential property of the Church to be so, because of her vocation to save men. Nowhere else does evil become so visible, because nowhere else is it

so keenly fought. "She can never work out of
the sphere of evil." As her Master came not
for the whole, but for the sick, so the Church
in this world will always have her sick, will
always have sores in her members, great and
small.[1]

The sinful members remain members of the
Church. In imitation of her master, the Church
does not will that a sinner be lost. She does not
deny those who deny her. She, the holy Church,
endures the sinners who are a burden on her
existence, defiling and disfiguring the purity of
her countenance.[2] And who is there in the
Church who would dare to say, "Lord, I give
thee thanks that I am not as these"? Which of
us would dare to maintain that he is not a part
of the lump of sin which weighs down the
Church? "For in many things we all offend"
(Jas. 3.2), and "If we say that we have no sin, we
deceive ourselves, and the truth is not in us."
(1 John 1.8.) The Church does not appoint a
group of Sinless Ones to recite the *Confiteor* on
behalf of sinners; it is the prayer of all. Priest

[1] Karl Adam, *The Spirit of Catholicism*, London,
1959, pp. 256–7.

[2] Cf. M. J. Scheeben, *The Mysteries of Christianity*,
St. Louis and London, 1954, p. 557; E. Mersch, *La
Théologie du Corps Mystique*, Paris, 1949, vol. 2,
pp. 231 ff.; Y. de Montcheuil, *Aspects de l'Eglise*, Paris,
1949, pp. 65–8; H. de Lubac, *Katholizismus als Gemein-
schaft*, Einsiedeln, 1943, pp. 60–9, 164 f.

and people alike must pray daily, "Forgive us our trespasses."

The sinner, as a *real person*, cannot be separated from the Church. Human reason can, indeed, make a meaningful distinction between a person *in so far* as he shares in Christ and the same person *in so far* as he is a sinner; and the concept of the Church refers primarily and directly to the first of these aspects: a person is a member of the Church in so far as he shares in Christ. But the wretchedness of the sinner as a member of the Church is precisely (as the Scriptures constantly make clear) that the Christian sinner cannot simply leave his wickedness, the sinful side of him, outside; he cannot split it off; the in-so-far-as-this and in-so-far-as-that cannot be understood and differentiated quantitatively. As one and the same indivisible human being with one and the same indivisible personality, the sinful Christian, in all his wretchedness, is a member of the Church.

In all ages—against the Gnostics, Novatians, Donatists and Montanists of the early centuries, against the Cathar movement in the Middle Ages, against the sectarians of the present day— the Church has in fact rejected the appeal to any supposed "Church of the pure". She knows that the Church is not a pure Platonic Idea, that here on earth there is no ideal Church. Hence the necessity of always looking at the Church

both from above *and* from below, both as
founded by God through Jesus Christ in the
Holy Spirit *and* as the assembly of the faithful
giving their consent to that divine decree, who
are ceaselessly engaged in making their community a reality from below upwards, and in
building it outwards into the world.

Even though the risen and glorified Lord
reign throughout the Church, she has not yet
reached her goal; here on her earthly pilgrimage it is rather the suffering, humiliated Lord
whose features she bears, though always in
that hope which is given her by the pledge of
the Spirit. Hence in speaking of the Church
we must always be careful to consider how
far, in any instance, we are seeing the power
of God at work in her, because of which the
gates of hell shall never prevail against her,
and how far we are faced with the "earthen
vessel" of her human form.[1]

But this does not present us with two
Churches: from above, the real, pure Church of
God, and from below, the impure Church of
men. There is *one* Church with two distinct
aspects which, while distinct, must both be
simultaneously given their full value. We should
be failing to give full value to the view from

[1] Cardinal Döpfner, "Kirche Christi unterwegs", in
Una Sancta, 12 (1957), 4.

above if we saw the Church only in terms of her members and so as ultimately only a human, indeed excessively human, social structure. We should be failing to give full value to the view from below if we saw her only in terms of her head, and so, ultimately, as already and without qualification an immaculate mystery of God in the Spirit.

We can indeed call the Church, even on earth, a Church "not having spot or wrinkle . . . holy and without blemish" (Eph. 5.27); we are then speaking of the glory with which, by God's grace, she is endowed from above, in her innermost depths, even in this world: the "pledge" of holiness. But the daily experience of the Church in the concrete will never allow us to forget that the Church "not having spot or wrinkle" is on this earth a *hidden* reality, not seen but, in the teeth of all her human wretchedness, believed. Her glory shines only for the believer: "Credo . . . sanctam ecclesiam." Only at the end of time (as we are assured not merely by modern exegetes but by the Fathers of the Church) will the Church without spot or wrinkle be an actual, total, manifest reality. To quote only two of the greatest Doctors of the Church:

> Wherever in my books I have described the Church as being without spot or wrinkle, it is not to be understood that she is so already, but that she is preparing herself to be so when

she too will appear in glory. For in the present time, because of much ignorance and weakness in her members, she must confess afresh each day "Forgive us our trespasses."[1]

That the Church may be glorious, without spot or wrinkle, is the final goal to which we are being led through the passion of Christ. It will be so only in our eternal home, not on our journey there, during which, if we said we had no sin we should be deceiving ourselves, as we are told in the first Epistle of St. John.[2]

Here, though Christ and the Church are one, lies the difference between the Church and her Lord. Like him, the Church on earth is in a state of humiliation; as in him, so in her, the divine has united itself with the human, indeed with the flesh; like him she can be, and like him she *has* been, tempted. But (this is the decisive difference) Christ alone, who became like unto

[1] Augustine, *Retractiones*, lib. 2, c. 18; *PL*, 32, 637 f.

[2] Thomas Aquinas, *Summa Theologica*, 3, q. 8, art. 3, ad 2.

For the exegetical history of Eph. 5.27, cf. C. Journet, *L'Eglise du Verbe incarné*, Paris, 1951, vol. 2, pp. 1115–29. However much we wish to refer the text to the Church here and now, we must in some sense concede that her purity will only be fully manifest at the end of time, and is in the meantime hidden under the form of a Church of sinners. While she is in this form she is an object of *faith*.

men in all else, is "without sin". (Heb. 4.15.) It is the misery of the Church, her chief suffering, that she can, in her members, yield to temptation.

The human form of Jesus is the pattern of the Church. He became true man in order to redeem men, and he founded his Church as a Church for men and of men. He never exempted the Church from human weakness. He did not predict that she would be in a state of perfection and final glory on her journey through history, but only at the end. If the Church is his body, then her visible bodiliness must reveal all the weakness which he himself showed upon earth, and this weakness needs must remain as a scandal throughout history. But while Jesus was sinless, *no* human weakness, including sin, is lacking in the men who form the community of the Church upon earth. Every human temptation which could ever lead men astray is possible to the members of the Church; not only to a part of the Church, or to a particular class of men, but simply to all Christians.[1]

A fully *adequate* concept of the Church will, then, include both sides of her: she is God's Church in her members. It includes at once

[1] P. Simon, *Das Menschliche in der Kirche Christi*, pp. 13 f.

what the Church receives from above, from
God's sanctifying grace through Christ in the
Spirit, and what the very same Church receives
and absorbs from below through her sinful members. The Church, adequately understood, is at
one and the same time the holy Church, the
holy bride, of Jesus Christ, and the Church of
sinners. Whatever the individual Christian does,
he does not do it only to his own personal profit
or loss. Rather, he does it as a member of the
Church fully responsible for the Church, for
good or ill. And so, because sinners are the real
members of the Church, and their sins remain
in her through her members, the Body of Christ
itself is burdened and stained with them; the
sins of men are the wounds of the Church.

Can we then call the Church of sinners a
"sinful Church"? Many theologians hesitate
here, and not without reason. It is an expression
that can be misunderstood; as though the grace
of God, the Holy Spirit in the Church, were not
pure and perfect, as though her divine constitution, coming from above, were not truly holy,
but in itself corrupt; as though the Church were
not set apart from the world as belonging to the
Lord, with the risen Christ and his Spirit active
in her ("church" being from the Greek *kyriake*,
"belonging to the Lord"); as though the Church
were not the new People of God, willing and
ready, believing and loving, but the unfaithful

Synagogue, unwilling and unworthy, herself
resisting God's choice of her.

We must not understand the expression "the
sinful Church" in any such way as this. All that
is good and holy, all that is of God, cannot but
remain what it is; the Church of God cannot
but remain God's Church. As coming from God,
the Church is and remains holy. Her holiness is
from Christ; she is holy not through the spirit
of her sinful members but through Christ's Holy
Spirit, not through their words and actions but
through Christ's doctrine and sacraments. But
it is precisely in seeing this that we must be
careful not to ignore or explain away the fright-
ful reality of sin in the Church, whose members,
inseparable from herself, are sinners. Obviously
it is not that the holiness and the sinfulness are
two equally valid aspects of the one Church.
The holiness is the light of the Church, the
sinfulness her shadow; the holiness reveals her
nature, the sinfulness obscures it. Sin does not
arise from the nature of the Church but breaks
into her from outside, through the power of the
Evil Spirit at work in men. Sin does not belong
to the nature of the Church but must be
reckoned as part of the unnatural condition in
which she is during her earthly pilgrimage.
To put it in the way in which it is usually put:
Sin in the Church is that *failure* in holiness
caused by the power of the Evil Spirit through

men as members of the Church. Sin in the Church, as part of the Church (as indeed elsewhere), can only be seen as a dark, incomprehensible, ultimately meaningless paradox. But as such it must be taken seriously. "Deus, qui ecclesiam tuam purificas"—"O God, who dost purify *thy Church*", we pray on the first Sunday in Lent. And on the fifteenth Sunday after Pentecost: "Let thy continual pity purify and defend thy Church; and because she cannot continue in safety without thee, direct her always by thy gracious help."

The idea of the holy Church, distinct from her often unholy members, mentally hypostatized into a sort of pure substance, is a dangerous abstraction. All too many good Christians are put off today by an idealizing type of speech and sermon about the faultless Church without reference to the concrete reality. But all too many will, on the other hand, excuse themselves from taking part in the life of the concrete reality of the holy Church on the ground that they accept the Church "in herself" (which is the abstract, "pure" Church again, perhaps "as she used to be") but not the Church "as she is". As though it were not the Christian's task to love the Church just *as she is*, in and in spite of the sinfulness of her members.

If we merely say, "Of course there are sinners in the Church, but this fact has nothing to do with the Church herself", then we are presupposing a highly questionable idealist notion of the Church, theologically speaking. The Church is then an idea, an ideal, something that is eventually to be, something to which appeal can be made from the concrete reality, something which is, as it were, only to be attained slowly, asymptotically, approximately. Of course one can always love such a thing as that, always give it one's allegiance; it is something invulnerable, untouched by the wretchedness of daily life. But it is not what is meant by the theological concept of the Church. According to this the Church is something real; the only Church there is, and in which we believe, is simply and always the visibly and hierarchically organized totality of the baptized, united in the external profession of faith and in obedience to the Roman Pope. And of this Church we simply cannot say that she has nothing to do with the sins of her members. Of course she does not approve their sins; of course there are people in her (and perhaps many such) who are in some true sense, which does not enter into this discussion, to be described as saints. But if she is something real, and if her members are sinners and, as sinners, remain her members, then she herself is sinful.

Then the sin of her children is a blot and a stain upon the holy mystical Body of Christ himself. The Church is a sinful Church: that is a truth of faith, not just a fact of her primitive experience. And it is a shattering truth.[1]

When we are concerned with the reform and renewal of the Church it would be particularly dangerous to see the evil in her as being only on the surface; it grows "not from", but "in her womb".[2] In so far as the body of the Church is divine and *human*, the human and all *too* human elements, actual sin and evil, can insinuate themselves into her; though without ever being able to overmaster her. This applies to ecclesiastical institutions and ordinances as well. Wherever men build their own institutions and ordinances on to the Church's divine ones, there sin can enter in and extend its domain; the holier the thing itself is, the greater the sin. The most visible and scandalous are naturally sins in association with ecclesiastical office, which, being a special gift, is a special temptation. The different degrees of the Church's hierarchy are not threatened only by the deformations of the historical process but also, and most

[1] Karl Rahner, S.J., *Kirche der Sünder,* Freiburg im Breisgau, 1948, pp. 14 f.

[2] M. J. Scheeben, *Mysterien*, p. 557.

deeply, by the personal sins of those who occupy
them as priests, as teachers, as shepherds.

Yet the "gates of hell", however we are to
understand them, cannot prevail against the
holy Church of God because her ultimate
stability is not in herself but in Jesus Christ
and the protection of his Holy Spirit. Essentially, she remains the true, the holy, the Church
who cannot, unlike the Synagogue, fall away
from grace and truth. Her innermost being—
Jesus Christ himself, his Spirit and his grace
—can never turn sinful; her innermost being,
her head, her life-principle and hence her
Gospel and her sacraments, are holy. Out of
regard for this fact it is better, after all, not to
call holy Church a "sinful Church", but in
general, to avoid misunderstanding, to prefer the
expression "the Church of sinners". But both
expressions can be misunderstood, the one as too
superficial, the other as too radical. Basically,
they correct one another. "The Church of
sinners" stresses that the sin is not in the Head
or the Spirit, not in any divine institution or
ordinance; the "sinful Church", that the sin in
the Church really does affect, oppress, wound
and deform the Church herself. Thus, according to Augustine, Psalm 103 calls upon the
Church, deformed by sin, to make her confession:

Do you wish to be pleasing to him [i.e., to Christ]?
You cannot, as long as you are deformed.
What will you do to be beautiful?
First let your deformity be displeasing to yourself, then you will merit beauty from him whom you wish to please with your beauty.
For he will reform you, who first formed you.

Notice Augustine's choice of words:

Vis ei placere?
Non potes, quamdiu *deformis* es; quid facies, ut pulchra sis?
Prius tibi displiceat *deformitas tua*, et tunc ab illo ipso cui vis placere pulchra, mereberis pulchritudinem.
Ipse enim erit *reformator* tuus, qui fuit *formator* tuus.[1]

The Church needs, not only one to form her in the first place, but always, because she is deformed, a *reformer*. And this is Christ himself. This is why, throughout everything that we must not shirk saying, in painful compassion and sorrowfully recognizing our co-responsibility, about the shadow-side of the Church, yet we can always firmly believe, in glad and unshakable faith, not in a sinful Church but in the

---

[1] Augustine, *Enarrationes in Psalmos*, Ps. 103, s. 1, 4 (*Corpus Christianorum*, AO, 1476).

holy Church. For Christ himself, through his Holy Spirit, ensures that the bright, invincible light of the Church's true nature will always in the end break through the darkness of her sinful un-nature.

But not without the co-operation of all of us as responsible members of her. Hence our conclusion is:

3. RENEWAL OF THE CHURCH IS ALWAYS NECESSARY

If we put together everything that we have said, or might have said, about the Church as made of men and of sinful men, everything that has happened in the Church's worldly and sinful history—the human, the all-too-human, the lethargy, the refusals, the mediocrity, the ill-will, the innocently-mistaken deviations and the actually sinful perversions—then only one thing remains to be done: *metanoia*, conversion of thought and deed. In so far as the Church is not only a divine institution but also a sociological human structure, in so far as God's holy Church is a Church of men and of sinful men, she, with everything that she is and has, is subject to that word of the Lord which reads "Do penance and be converted." In so far as the Church is deformed, she has to be reformed: *ecclesia reformanda*.

And in so far as the Church, because of her human frailty and sinfulness, always needs to be better; in so far as she can never sit and bask in the warmth of her own self-satisfaction but must always be pressing on with all the earnest zeal of the penitent—this renewal of the Church is never something finished and done with but is always a permanent duty: and this precisely because she is, and is to remain, the *holy* Church. In so far as the Church is constantly, repeatedly deformed, she has to be constantly, repeatedly reformed: *ecclesia semper reformanda.*

But reform is necessary not only because of deformation. Fundamentally, it is not just a negative matter of house-cleaning and repairs, but a vast positive task of constructive building. It is not only because there are mistaken developments and mistaken attitudes in the Church that she has this task. Even if there were none (there always will be) the Church would still have the great task of renewal. For the mustard-seed must grow. The Church, as we said at the beginning of this chapter, is in the stream of time: she has to keep adopting new forms, new embodiments. She has to keep giving herself a new form, a new shape in history; she is never simply finished and complete. She must go into all the world and preach the good news to every creature (Mark 16.15); to all nations, to all cultures, to all ages, until

Christ comes again. Such is her incomparably happy mission. Hence she is forever faced afresh with the task of renewing herself. Hence, again, this renewal is not just something which she stringently *must* do, but which she joyously *may* do; a joyful service to the Kingdom of God, looking towards him who will make *all* things new, a new heaven and a new earth. The Pope's summons to renew the Church is, most solemnly and truly, a joyful summons.

We have so far been exploring the theological grounds for saying *that* the Church must be renewed. From this basis we can go on to consider *how* it is to be done.

3. THE FRAMEWORK FOR CATHOLIC RENEWAL

THERE is true reform and false reform. The Pope intends that the Council, with the reunion of separated Christians in mind, shall undertake a true reform; in fact, a genuine renewal. Hence not only the assembled bishops but all the members of the Church are to have their task in this great work. This is why the Pope himself takes every possible opportunity of speaking to every kind of group about this desire of his heart. It is only if the Council becomes the concern of the whole Church that it can succeed in the way the Pope wishes. For this reason we must make a thorough theological enquiry into the possibilities and limits of Catholic renewal. What may we, as Christians, do? "May", not merely in the external sense of what is morally permissible, but in the deeper sense of what is according to the gift of grace?

1. WE CAN SUFFER

We can suffer because of the failures and sins in the Church as she now is. The Pope's call for a renewal of the Church as a condition for re-union must be understood as having a bearing

on this suffering. We do not need to put on any
act of denominational optimism, to put up a
front of apologetics, to hand out nothing to the
Press but victory communiqués. We are not
obliged to act before the world as though everything were for the best with us. We can display
our poverty, our wretchedness, our shame. We
can allow our suffering really to pierce to the
heart, our suffering over the Church as she is,
unrenewed, unreformed; the greatest saints,
such as Bernard of Clairvaux, Catherine of
Siena, Teresa of Avila, Clemens Maria Hofbauer, and countless others, have been the ones
who suffered from it most of all.

It would be a very odd sort of Christian who
could survey his Church from the outside with
detached indifference or from the inside with
cosy contentment. He would certainly not be
what St. Paul sees as a living, feeling, participat-
ing member of the body of Christ. There is such
a thing, among both clergy and laity, as a false
contentment with the Church, a false pride in
the Church, a false enthusiasm for the Church.
It is the product (when not due to excusable
ignorance) of a far from excusable superficial,
illusory, often even frivolously presumptuous
assessment of the situation of the Church in the
world. This mentality, with its familiar bro-
mides—"It's not that bad", "It's always been
so", "We just mustn't exaggerate", "Pensiamo

in secoli!"—could, if widespread, seriously
hinder the renewal of the Church.

But it would be an equally odd sort of Christian who felt no guilt in himself for the failures
and sins of the Church, who was not painfully
aware that he is constantly revealing himself as
an unreformed member of the Church to be
reformed. When he looks in humility and shame
at himself, he will be all the more ready to
practise that virtue which is especially necessary
for a renewal of the Church; namely, patience.

Anyone who has never, as a member of the
Church, suffered on account of his Church, has
never known her as she really is or never loved
her. Genuine suffering on account of the Church
springs from love of the Church; love for a
Church who is too unlike her Lord. This loving
suffering makes it possible to endure many un-
endurable things about the poor Church as she
is in the world of time, and even to make them
fruitful. Because this suffering springs from
love, love for the Church and her Lord, it is not
without fruit for the Church. For why should
it not be especially true of this suffering, suffering on account of the Church, that it serves for
the building up of the body of Christ? Let us,
then, in this special suffering fill up those things
that are wanting of the sufferings of Christ, in
our flesh, for his Body, which is the Church.
(Col. 1.24.) Thus this seemingly useless *passio*
on account of the Church will, if we live through

it aright, become an *actio*, a source of blessings for the Church. Suffering turns to grace.

To turn our thoughts now towards reunion: What have we a right to expect from our separated brethren? What can we expect from each other? The sharing of suffering. This in three ways:

(a) Suffering *with* those who are *not* of our communion; not open or concealed pleasure in their embarrassments, but honest sympathy. Yet how many Christians there still are who will, with a certain (unacknowledged) satisfaction, take up the weaknesses, disasters and scandals of another communion—real or unreal, doctrinal or practical—and talk about them, preach about them, publish them, in a ruthless sectarian display of detraction or downright calumny!

(b) Suffering with each other on account of our own Church; not denominational self-satisfaction, but anxious awareness of the condition and the shortcomings of our own Church. Yet how many Christians there still are who are able to see and deplore disorders only in someone else's house, never in their own, who want to unload all the guilt from themselves on to the other side, and who seem to think that all the disputes in the Church would be settled if only their brethren in the other house would come over into their own "well-ordered" one.

(c) Suffering *with* each other over the fact of schism: not bored acceptance of the situation but painfully felt involvement in it. Schism is a scandal. But it is perhaps an even greater scandal that a majority of Christians in all communions, even today, and including theologians and pastors, are profoundly indifferent to this scandal; that they feel the division of Christendom at most as a deplorable imperfection, not as an immeasurably crippling, gaping wound which absolutely must be healed; that they are deeply concerned over a thousand religious trivialities, but not over our Lord's desire just before his death "that they may all be one". Will the words and actions of the Pope be enough to awaken these sleepers?

2. WE CAN PRAY

We can pray for deliverance from evil. As Christians, whose hope is in God's grace, we shall not think that *we* can, by our *own* power, renew the face of the earth and of the Church. It is the Spirit who will form all things anew. The daily prayer of Christians in the Church, for the Church and not least for themselves, will be *Veni, Sancte Spiritus*:

> What is filthy, do thou wash,
> What is dry, do thou refresh,
> What is wounded, do thou heal;
> What is rigid, do thou bend,
> What is frozen, do thou melt,
> What is wandering, do thou rule.

In Christians, suffering because of the Church will of itself turn to prayer for the Church. Prayer for the Church to be delivered from evil, and so to be renewed, will not be just one additional thing to be done; it will be the *first* thing to be done, before any reforming action, which must in fact flow from it. This because everything depends upon God's grace. Reforming activism without prayer is a mill without water. In this sense everyone—including the simple "ordinary Catholic" who thinks he is not wanted in such a matter—has the opportunity to help in the renewal of the Church. It would be a great ground for hope if, at this momentous time, many of those prayers which are narrowly focused upon purely personal needs were to be turned outwards to become part of the great petitions of the universal Church, and especially if they were for the Ecumenical Council, for which the Pope keeps asking for prayers.

And what can we reasonably expect from our separated fellow-Christians, from each other? That they pray with us. That we should all alike pray that other communions, and our own, be delivered from evil, and especially that we be delivered from the evil of schism; that all pre-judice and ignorance on both sides be removed, that misunderstandings be cleared up, errors recognized, mistrust, suspicion and estrangement overcome; that each communion should have the courage to recognize its own share of guilt for the schism, and publicly acknowledge and atone for its guilt; that we shall manage to forgive each other, that we shall take every possible step towards each other, that we shall not give up hope . . .

Praying together means, in the concrete:

(a) Not praying *against* each other; not, like the sons of Zebedee, asking that we should have, or keep, the principal places we have so well deserved, and that the others should come *after* us! Nor like the Pharisee in the Temple, arrogantly giving thanks that we are not as the rest of men; that we have done, or not done, this and that which "the others" have omitted or committed; that it is not we, but the others, who have to be converted. From the fact that the others have something decisive to do it does not follow that we have *nothing* decisive to do.

(b) Praying *for* each other; not just in general, but in particular: Catholics for their Protestant brethren, Protestants for their Catholic brethren (not forgetting the Eastern Church, which happens to be geographically further off). And Catholics for the leaders of the Protestant Churches, and Protestants for the Catholic bishops and the Pope. And this prayer is to be, not a disagreeable duty but an expression of all-embracing love. And let not those be forgotten who are very apt indeed to be ignored,

those of whom Archbishop Lorenz Jaeger of
Paderborn spoke in his pastoral for the Unity
Octave in 1958: "Our prayers are specially
needed by those learned theologians who are
working in the field of controversy, who are
responsibly and courageously clarifying ideas
and trying to clear away the débris of centuries
of polemic." Let us then pray specially for them
to the Holy Spirit: that they take their stand
not on schools of thought but on the Gospel of
Christ, that they may have no desire to "win"
in controversy, that truth and love be wholly
identified in them, that they should strive not to
perpetuate differences but to resolve them, that
their heart's desire should be not the drawing
of frontiers but the finding of common ground
. . . Finally, praying for each other also means,
in the concrete, praying for the Ecumenical
Council: it is a concern of *all* Christians.

(c) Making it our common prayer that not our
own but God's will be done. It is possible to
have some definite, all-too-human mental image
of reunion, and then to pray, consciously or
unconsciously, that reunion may happen like
that. We shall, on the contrary, pray that reunion may happen as and when *God* wills.

In all our prayer, we must have confidence;
the faith which can move mountains, which
does not relegate reunion, as an "insoluble problem", to the outcome of history or to the Last

Day, but which, hoping against all hope (Rom. 4.18), trusts fully that "all things whatsoever you ask when ye pray, believe that you shall receive, and they shall come unto you." (Mark 11.24.)

3. WE CAN CRITICIZE

While we suffer and pray, we do not have to give our assent and amen to *everything* in the Church. Criticism, indeed loud criticism, can be a duty. A Christian will spontaneously recognize the good that there is in the Church and rejoice over it. He knows too that there is a time to speak and a time to be silent, and finally that every thing and every act, even every reforming and renewing act, has its *kairos*, its "due time".

But he will not side with those who hold, out of naive self-satisfaction, or cowardly servility, or mere contentment with things as they are disguised as loyalty to the Church, that everything must be approved or excused; who take every criticism of the Church as a damnable attack upon God himself; who even try to repress all criticism, which merely means that they conjure up still more dangerous forces of compensation or rebellion. A vague, undefined discontent is hurtful; specific criticism is liberating and fruitful.

As a Church of *men*, sinful men, the Church, though of divine foundation, *needs* criticizing;

3*

as the Church of *God* she is, more than any other institution, *worth* criticizing. To show by criticism what has become humanly deformed in the Church is a necessary preliminary to any reform. How can failures and abuses be corrected if they cannot be spoken of and discussed? How can we ever do without those who put into words what needs to be said if the Church is to make spiritual progress, what many others are thinking and because of which they are suffering? "Brethren, extinguish not the Spirit! Despise not inspired speech! But prove all things, hold fast that which is good. From all appearance of evil refrain yourselves." (1 Thess. 5.19–22.)

There has always been criticism in the Church. The Fathers were capable of expressing themselves severely on the subject of abuses. Pope Gregory the Great laid down the important principle that "if scandal is taken at the truth, then it is better to allow scandal to arise than to abandon the truth."[1] During the Middle Ages, up to the beginning of the Reformation, criticism within the Church was the order of the day. To cite only two representative examples: Bernard of Clairvaux's *De Consideratione,* written for Pope Eugenius III, and the *Tractatus de Modo Concilii Generalis Celebrandi et Corruptelis in Ecclesia Reformandis* of William Durandus, Bishop of Mende, presented to the Council of Vienne.

[1] Gregory the Great, *In Ezech. Hom.* 7, *PL,* 77, 324.

Thomas Aquinas treats of important aspects of criticism within the Church, in so far as it can have a personal bearing, under the title of *correctio fraterna*, to which he devoted an entire eight-article *quaestio* in the *Summa Theologica*;[1] *correctio* would be well translated, for our times, as "constructive criticism". Fraternal criticism, properly understood, is for St. Thomas an act of love, even more than the healing of a physical injury would be (art. 1); it is, basically, a duty (art. 2) of those in subordinate as well as of those in authoritative positions in the Church (art. 3). To the explicit question, whether one must correct and criticize one's ecclesiastical superior (*praelatus*), Thomas answers, "Fraternal criticism, which is an act of love, is a matter for everyone in regard to anyone whatsoever whom he is meant to love; always providing that there is something present which needs to be criticized"; but "in criticism of an ecclesiastical superior by a subordinate, an appropriate manner of criticism must be used; it must not be impudent and harsh but mild and respectful." (art. 4.) And to the difficulty, advanced in connection with Gal. 2.11, that one who is not the equal (*par*) of an ecclesiastical authority may not criticize him, St. Thomas answers, "But one must realize that where there is danger to the Faith, one who is in authority in the Church is to be rebuked even publicly. And so Paul, who was

[1] 2-2, q. 33, arts. 1-8.

subject to Peter, rebuked Peter publicly because of a danger of scandal which was a threat to the Faith. And as Augustine observes in his gloss on Gal. 2.14, Peter himself has given an example to those in high places, that in any case where they may have strayed from the right way, they should not be ashamed to take criticism even from those of lower rank." (art. 4 ad 2.)

It is only when we come to modern times, after the debates with the Reformation, with Gallicanism, the Enlightenment, the French Revolution and nineteenth-century Liberalism, that we find a series of violent, ruthless attacks, such as threaten her very existence, driving the Church into a permanently defensive and pugnacious attitude in which she is constantly touchy about criticism. There is a difference between the Middle Ages, which had, at bottom, a positive attitude to ecclesiastical authority, and the modern world, which is not only outside the Church but against the Church. There is a difference between Bernard of Clairvaux, who publicly rebuked the Pope while remaining loyal to him, and Luther, who cared nothing for the Church's excommunication; a difference between Dante, who placed three Popes, including Boniface VIII, then living, in hell, but was still faithful to the Papacy and the Church, and Voltaire, who damned the Church herself; a difference between the criticisms of medieval universities and Imperial Diets and the criticisms of the unbelieving scholars and politicians of the nineteenth century.

But after two world wars, the Church in the Western world is no longer the object of these furious general attacks; her position today is not only strong enough to be able to bear criticism, but would actually be strengthened by self-criticism. It is an encouraging sign of the Church's vitality in our day that criticism is now heard less from the bitter, aloof outsider or the abusive enemy of the Church, whether stupid or intelligent, and more from those (setting aside the whiners and grumblers found in every age) who are loyal members of her, who are distinguished by their deep sense of responsibility, their unselfish readiness to commit themselves, their courageous initiative. There is a good Catholic tradition to which they can appeal, a long series of great Catholic critics, unbroken all down the centuries. Criticism was offered not only by Paul to Peter, but by Jerome to Pope Damasus, by Columbanus to Boniface IV, by Bernard of Clairvaux and Gerhoh of Reichersberg to Eugenius II, by Bridget of Sweden to Gregory XI, by Philip Neri to Clement VIII, not forgetting Catherine of Siena, Bernardine of Siena, Thomas More, Robert Bellarmine, Clement Maria Hofbauer . . . And all these famous names stand for innumerable unknown

ones, men and women who acknowledged the
holiness of the Church but who brought forward
their criticisms in their own day without making
any comfortable appeal to her visible holiness.

Must not self-criticism in the Church be
especially necessary in this present age—an age
in which the common men, "the masses", are
entering into full participation in the life of
the Church, and in which collectivism and
totalitarianism, in various disguises, are making
their way into the Church as well as elsewhere?
Repression of criticism has always been and is a
characteristic of totalitarian states, a sign not of
strength but of weakness and fear. Pius XII
emphatically asserted the necessity for a critical
public opinion in the Church, against all doubtful and fearful souls, in his address to the International Catholic Press Congress in Rome in
February 1950:

> We should like to add a word about public
> opinion within the Church (within those
> areas, of course, where there is room for free
> discussion). This can be a matter of surprise
> only to those who do not know the Church or
> who know her badly. For she is a living body,
> and something would be lacking to her life
> if public opinion were lacking. This would
> be a defect which would be a reproach alike
> to her pastors and to the faithful.[1]

[1] *Osservatore Romano,* 18 Feb. 1950.

Public opinion in the Church, and the toleration of it, must not remain a purely theoretical postulate.

But all this gives no licence to an unchristian criticism of the Church. Criticism is Christian when it starts not from resentment against the Church (or the clergy) but from gratitude to the Church, and even the clergy; there is always more occasion for thankfulness in the Catholic Church than for blame. Criticism of the Church is Christian when its ultimate root is *love* for the Church.

Criticism based on love will be *restrained*: one will combine criticism of others with a humble criticism of one's own weaknesses; offer one's criticism for counter-criticism; criticize sometimes by speaking, sometimes by keeping silence; will not go beyond one's competence; will distinguish between essentials and inessentials; and will be in all things intelligent, fair and balanced.

Criticism based on love will be *committed*, committed to the Church: one will not speak as from some unattainable distance, but always as a member of the Church, always with a sense of brotherly unity with the other members and, ultimately, with reverence; one will criticize the Church never from a secular, neutral, detached point of view but always from an ecclesiastical, co-responsible point of view. Out of the depth of one's commitment, in fact. No one who simply "practises", without committing himself, can be a convincing critic. It is all too easy for the man on the bank to tell you how to swim.

Criticism based on love will be *constructive*: one will not go in for bad-tempered grumbling, sterile fault-finding, fundamentally and exclusively negative criticism for criticism's sake, but produce positive, constructive criticisms. One will not be intent on tracking down abuses, whether with delight or disgust, but will be trying to establish norms.

And what can we expect here from our separated fellow-Christians, from each other? Co-operative criticism. Primarily, this means becoming aware of the duty of a discerning and constructive criticism within one's own communion. Does it also mean criticism of each other's communions? This is a risky business, most often clumsily and unreasonably performed and ill-understood; none of us wants to go back to the age of sterile sectarian polemics from which we have only just escaped. Are we, then, going to criticize other bodies of believers from the outside? But, when we really come down to it, it is still from the inside. The "others" are not simply strangers, simply others. It is not that they do *not* believe, it is that they believe *differently*; that is, they too are Christians, who wish to believe in the same Christ and his

Gospel, but believe in it *differently* (and, as we have to say, mistakenly). It is this that makes everything so difficult. We are everywhere involved in a different interpretation of one and the same Gospel, with both sides assuming, necessarily assuming, that *their* interpretation is the right one.

A simply condemnatory criticism is, then, since other Christians believe in the same Gospel, out of the question. Special care will be needed when criticizing "the others", since it may often emerge, after closer examination, that they believe the same thing in the very same way, though expressed perhaps with different words and concepts. For choice, then, a Christian will simply ask his fellow-Christians critical *questions*, with a reference to the one Gospel of Christ. How do you understand this element in the Gospel, or that one? Have you considered this other point, as well? In what way do you act according to it? With questions such as these we can hold the mirror of Christ's Gospel up to one another, as a test both of them and of ourselves. In this way, the things that we regard as essential requirements are brought home to them, and at the same time we are given the possibility of a new critical insight into our own teaching and life, which will lead to a meeting on our part of *their* essential requirements —all with reunion as the ultimate goal. We

Catholics, then, expect Protestants to ask us critical questions of this sort, and we shall ask them in return. We Catholics expect them especially now, before the Ecumenical Council which is to serve the cause of reunion: such questions as will reveal the truth through love.

4. WE CAN ACT

We can suffer, we can pray and, however much we criticize, we can hope for the glory of the Kingdom of God, which is not granted to us in this age and will only be given to us, by the Lord himself, at the end of time; it is only when "God will be all in all" (1 Cor. 15.28) that the Church will be utterly without spot or wrinkle. But hoping does not mean sitting with idle hands, lazily waiting, in the way for which St. Paul scolds the Thessalonians. It is not by sterile complaints and idle criticisms, scattered ideas or resounding speeches about what we might or may or should or must do, that anything in fact gets *done*.

So, we can act. When it comes to abuses in the Church, the sum total of being a Catholic does not consist in swallowing them, though Karl Barth once wondered if it did. You swallow down the nasty mouthful, he supposed, take a deep breath, and declare that it's true enough, but you're a staunch Catholic for all that; and that is *all*. We cannot agree with him. At the very least, the swallowing-down (which can sometimes be necessary in non-Catholic circles, too) has to be complemented by action; there has to be a decisive *agere contra* which, if it is to be fruitful, must at the same time be an *agere pro*. Such action must not stop short at purely negative abolitions, condemnations and prohibitions, but be a positive renewal of form and structure. It must be a cheerful carrying out of Christ's missionary command to his Church, a command which requires her to renew her forms and structures tirelessly in every age, so as to present herself in such a way as to win belief. This is why, in Catholic circles, the word "renewal" is always preferred to the word "reform", because it stresses the positive and creative aspect. Catholic reform, being renewal, is neither innovation nor restoration. Pius X's motto of "renewing all things in Christ" was expressed neither by "innovare omnia in Christo" nor by "restaurare omnia in Christo" but by "instaurare omnia in Christo".

And this is how the present Pope, as we have already seen, regards the task of the Ecumenical Council: a positive renewal (*renovatio*) and adaptation (*accomodatio*) of the Church to present needs and conditions, or, to use the Italian word which expresses it so accurately, an *aggiornamento*, a bringing-up-to-the-present-day.[1] How, basically, is this to be understood? Catholic reform, being renewal, lies midway between two extremes, revolution and restoration.

Catholic reform is *not revolution*: it does not aim at the violent overthrow either of values or of authority; it is not bent upon what is new in a doctrinaire, fanatical fashion, without piety towards the past. While fully aware of what is better in what is new, Catholic reform is intent upon preserving the continuity of historical development, and hence is not innovation but *renewal*.

Catholic reform is *not restoration*; it does not aim lethargically at the maintenance of a system but courageously advances towards ever greater truth. It has no wish to re-establish old forms, but to discover new forms appropriate to the times. It does not wish to tighten up the rigorous observance of laws, regulations, canons and subsections and so revive some outworn disciplinary system, but to renew the Church's institutions

[1] Cf., besides the original encyclical, the Pope's address to the Oriental College and the description of the objects of the Council by Cardinal Tardini, Cardinal Secretary of State: "The increase of the Catholic faith, a healthy renewal of the morals of the Christian people, the *aggiornamento* of ecclesiastical discipline according to the needs of the times". (*Osservatore Romano*, 1 Nov. 1959.)

from within. While fully aware of the value of ancient tradition, Catholic reform is intent upon that creative renewal of the Church's structure which the present demands. Hence it is not simply restoration but *renewal*.

Reform as envisaged with reference to the coming Council is to be a renewal of the Church, an adaptation of the Church and her discipline to the demands of the present day. The Pope has in this connection spoken explicitly of ecclesiastical discipline and of the modernization of pastoral work. This excludes two further misunderstandings: Catholic reform, being a renewal, is neither a purely interior reform of the heart nor a purely exterior reform of abuses. Obviously, it is right to expect everyone to begin the reform *in himself*; reform of the Church cannot be a matter of academic discussion. But anyone who thinks it can be done with an interior, moral change of heart alone is ignoring the concrete reality. The good dispositions and intentions of the heart are not enough. Only too often good will is present in an individual and cannot achieve anything. Why? Because the outward conditions, means, forms and structures of the Church make the achievement of his good intention difficult or even impossible. Many good Catholics would gladly have received the Eucharist more often, but it was only when the over-strict fasting laws were abolished that they were able to do so; they needed a change in Church discipline.

An interior change of heart is not enough, but nor is an exterior reform of abuses. Of course, a great deal has been done once the abuses in some institution or regulation have been removed. But it is possible for some institution to be restored and yet to be, because times have changed, either non-viable or at least inadequately effective. The removal by the Council of Trent of abuses in the celebration of the Mass had only a limited effect until the liturgy was creatively renewed (at least within certain limits), as in the community Mass in Germany or the new liturgy of Holy Week: i.e., in the sense of a positive renewal, an *aggiornamento*, a modernization of the pastoral approach.

A reform of the Church which is neither revolution nor restoration, neither a mere change of heart nor a mere reform of abuses, could be described either as a creative reform of the state of the Church, or, again, as a renewal. The French Dominican Yves Congar has made a thorough and detailed study of the problems of such a reform: we are especially indebted to him for the stimulating and essential ideas contained in these four points, in which he is prudently indicating the principles of a "reform without schism":

(a) That we must give priority to charity and pastoral considerations.

(b) That we must remain a part of the whole community.

(c) That we must both have patience and avoid delays.

(d) That we must carry out a real renewal by returning to the sources of things and to tradition, not by introducing innovations by way of a merely mechanical adaptation.[1]

But is there not a danger that such a reform of the state of the Church will attack something essential in her? Is there not anything in the Church that is absolute? There is indeed, but even in the Church the relative is not to be made absolute. On the contrary, the absolute and the relative, the essential nature and its working out in history, though they cannot be separated, even outwardly, must be clearly distinguished. Catholic reform cannot take place in the sphere of the absolute, the essence of Catholicism; it occurs in that of the relative, the working out at the historical level. The liturgy, the apostolate, the doctrine of the Catholic Church—which are essential to her are immersed, as to their concrete forms, in history, and are to this extent, as we have indicated, subject to culpable or inculpable historical deformations; and must therefore, to this extent, be constantly reformed and renewed.

[1] Yves Congar, O.P., *Vraie et fausse réforme dans l'Église*, Paris, 1950, pp. 231–352.

But how is this inviolable "essence" to be described? We have to distinguish between what is directly of divine institution (which may yet include a human element in it) and what is directly of human institution. The essence is, in this sense, what belongs to the divine economy of salvation, i.e., what God, through Jesus Christ, gave to the Church for her journey down the centuries. What God, through Christ, in the Holy Spirit, set up and established in the Church shares in the indefectible perfection and holiness of God and is in no need of reform. But what men set up and establish on the basis of this divine institution and establishment shares in the imperfection and sinfulness of man and is always in need of reform. Jesus Christ saw the dangers which threaten the Church from below, from the infernal world. So he built the Church upon rock, gave her a message, a structure, and equipment against which that infernal world can do nothing. But he did not take her out of this world. The Church will always preserve her master's message, but members of the Church, and individual groups, can corrupt it by heretical error or, for that matter, pseudo-orthodox aridity and onesidedness. The Church will always preserve the organizational form which she received from Christ, but life within that organizational form can, in the concrete, be led in a manner contrary to the meaning of the organization itself and to the will of its founder.

From this it is clear that we cannot simply speak of "irreformable areas" of the Church, as though there were two storeys of a building, one on top of the other, of which one was reformable and the other irreformable; as though it were possible adequately to separate off the irreformable essence of the Church's institutions, as established by God, from the concrete working-out of them and the living structure given to them by men in the history of the Church. It is rather that the essence is embedded in the human working-out in history somewhat as the plan, and the permanent principles of architecture and engineering, enter into the actual concrete building. Every part of the building, even the innermost room in it, or the most important or the most valuable, is, basically, liable to need renewing and can therefore be reformed and renewed. Only, the plan as expressed in any particular part of the building, and the laws of construction, as they apply to it, must not be set aside; no part of the building must become simply something else, or collapse altogether. Every institution, even the very holiest (the celebration of the Eucharist, or the preaching of the Gospel), every aspect of organization (even the primacy of Rome, or the episcopal government of the Church) can, through the historical process of formation and deformation, come to need renewal, and must then be reformed and renewed; only, the basic irreformable pattern given by God through Christ must not be set aside. Indeed, the holier the institution, the worse the damage, and the more urgent the renewal; think of the disastrous confusion of tradition with "traditional" (but perhaps extremely recent) customs; of orthodoxy with conformism, of the discipline of the Church with legalism, of veneration for Mary with Marianism, of ecclesiastical institutions with institutionalism, of sacraments with sacramentarianism, of the Papacy with papalism, and so forth. The task of Catholic renewal will be not only to avoid damaging the essence of any institution given by God through Christ, but to bring it more to the fore, so that its working out at the historical level shall not obscure it but let it shine out. What things are to be corrected by reform is one important question; but just as important is this other: In what direction, towards what *forma*, in the deepest sense of the word, shall reform proceed? For it is only if it has the result described above that it is really a positive renewal.

But according to what *norm* shall action for the renewal of the Church be measured? There is only one norm whose authority is adequate. There is no ordinary human norm which can measure every institution in the Church, Pope, bishops, priests and laity, the whole Church of yesterday, today and tomorrow. The norm to which we can keep looking, in all our action, is Jesus Christ, the Lord of the Church, who speaks to the Church of every century in his Gospel, making his demands upon her. The tradition of the Church will help us to understand the Gospel of Jesus Christ aright; and it is the apostolic Church, which was especially near her Lord, which gave us the canon of Scripture, the Scriptures themselves and Church government in its first form, which, through an understanding of Christ's Gospel, will provide us in a special sense with a model (though not one to be mechanically copied) for renewal of the Church. It is, in fact, a matter of acting according to the Gospel. We can be fearlessly confident that the *vox Evangelii*, being the *vox Dei*, will also be the best possible answer to the *vox temporis*. Neither opportunist modernism nor opportunist traditionalism but fidelity to the Gospel of Jesus Christ is the right frame of mind for a renewal of the Church.

Loyalty to the Gospel involves loyalty to the Church who preaches the Gospel to us. *Sentire in Ecclesia*, thinking in the Church (which is the original Ignatian idea, rather than the less exact *sentire cum Ecclesia*, thinking with the Church), is an essential requirement for any reforming action. Renewal of the Church must not be revolution, must not lead out of the Church but deeper into her. Hence it must be carried out in a genuine, loyal, honest, free *obedience* to the Church's leaders, whose duty it is to feed the flock and in whose voice we hear the voice of the Lord. Obedience, which always involves self-denial, will mean that one will often do something for the good of the whole which, if left to oneself, one would not have done; and will leave undone much that, if left to oneself, one would have done. One will often be silent when one would like to speak, wait when one would like to hurry, serve when one would like to put on pressure, pray when one would like to grumble. In short, one will obey, and so demonstrate precisely the *liberty* of a Christian man, a follower of Jesus Christ himself. Obedience to him, to whom alone as free Christians our obedience is due, becomes a concrete reality in the Church. All this has absolutely nothing to do with the pernicious principle that "orders is orders", making those in authority arbitrary and depriving those under it of all responsibility. Ecclesiastical obedience is not according to the letter that killeth but the spirit that quickeneth. True obedience is rooted in a loving faith and confidence (both in those who hold authority and those who are under it) in the workings of the Holy Spirit, who animates the *whole* Church.

A reverent recognition by the faithful of the action of the Spirit in those who teach and rule in the Church, and a reverent recognition by those holding office of the activity of the same Spirit guiding every single believer in his religious decisions, will give us the secret of overcoming many conflicts. Confidence in the Spirit at work in the individual believer safeguards the man in authority against that "responsibility complex" which tends to surround all that the faithful are to do or not to do with cramping restrictions, so as to ensure its total dependence on himself. Similarly, confidence in the Spirit at work in the exercise of the teaching and pastoral office safeguards the individual believer from seeing papal and episcopal directives and leadership as a shockingly patronizing restriction of his rights as an adult, to be countered by an appeal to his personal conscience. We can see from this that, in both, Christian freedom is the conquest of exaggerated fear; fear of how daring freedom may become, and fear of how authority may be misused, are both only a lack of faith and a lack of courage. They overrate the human element in the Church and underrate the divine element in her.[1]

Ecclesiastical obedience never does anything contrary to conscience. We do not in the Church, any more than elsewhere, have "blind obedience", but that obedience which "proves all things". (Cf. 1 Thess. 5.21.)

It is only as free obedience that obedience is a moral act, not as the purely external fulfilment of some external order. Obedience is valid only if the person of whom obedience is demanded has fully the right to examine whether the command is valid, in particular with reference to the competence of the person giving it. Even in ecclesiastical circles, this competence may be overstepped sometimes. In such a case, it is not disloyalty to the Church to refuse obedience.

Again, it is bound to happen in the very nature of things that a person exercising authority from above will sometimes have a less complete knowledge of the situation with which he is dealing than the person whose obedience he demands. It is part of traditional Catholic moral theology that a person thus summoned to obedience can, may, and in some circumstances even must refrain from

[1] H. Hirschmann, S.J., "Die Freiheit in der Kirche", in *Stimmen der Zeit* 161 (1957–8), 85 f.

carrying out the directive if after careful consideration he comes to the conclusion that the
one who gave the order, if he saw it from
where he himself sees it, would not insist
upon it.[1]

True ecclesiastical obedience unites subject
and superior in a common responsibility, serving the true liberty of a Christian man. Thus
reform of the Church will always be an act of
obedience and freedom, an act of Christians
who are free in their obedience and obedient
in their freedom.

And what can we expect from our separated
fellow-Christians, from each other? That they
act with us. We have already said, in the introductory chapter, that direct, formal, equal participation and negotiation in the deliberations
of the Council would not at this time achieve
anything or even be desirable. What four hundred years of misunderstanding and alienation
have built up between Catholics and Protestants
cannot be demolished in relatively short negotia-
tions. But this really does not mean that we are

[1] Hirschmann, "Freiheit", 88 f. On the theology of
obedience, cf. Karl Rahner, S.J., "Eine ignationische
Grundhaltung. Marginalien über den Gehorsam", in
Stimmen der Zeit, 158 (1955-6), 253-67; *Sendung und
Gnade*, Innsbruck, 1959, pp. 493-516; "Freiheit in der
Kirche", in *Schriften zur Theologie*, Ensiedeln, 1955,
2, 95-114; *Free Speech in the Church*, London, 1960.

to stand idly waiting; on the contrary, our most important task at the moment, on both sides, is reforming action within our own communion —reforming action according to the same norm, which is the Gospel of Jesus Christ. No denomination would dare to assert that it is, in its whole life and activity, exactly proportioned to its own ultimate standard, which is the Gospel. No denomination would even dare to assert that it is so proportioned to the degree which others would reasonably have a right to expect of it. This calls for action within one's own communion, which will be in fact a co-operation with other communions. If Catholics and Protestants both try, while bearing each other in mind, to get closer and closer to their own standards, then (since the standard is the same for both) they and their basic demands must begin more and more to coincide with each other. And at once this common reforming action within our own communion will become more and more an interchange of action and negotiation with one another.

Such, then, is the framework for a Catholic renewal; this is what we may, with God's grace, do: in the cause of renewal we can suffer, pray, criticize, and above all act; not for revolution, not for restoration, not for a mere change of heart nor a mere reform of abuses, but for a creative reform of the state of the Church. And

all this within our own Church and for our own
Church, but at the same time with and for our
separated brethren. The ancient basilica is not
to be torn down and rebuilt, but nor is it merely
to be scrubbed down, patched up and dusted
off; it is to be, in accordance with the ancient
plan of its founder, but for the needs of this new
age, *renewed*. Such is Catholic reform. Fine, in
theory. What of the reality?

4. RENEWAL OF THE CHURCH, PAST AND PRESENT

THE coming Ecumenical Council will not be the beginning of renewal in the Catholic Church. She has been repeatedly working at it for a long time. The Catholic Church has her *chronique scandaleuse*; it is serious, it is tragic, but it is ultimately uninteresting to this extent, that it is all to be found as much outside the Catholic Church as inside her—wherever there are human beings, in fact. But along with it there is also the incomparably more interesting chronicle of the *ecclesia catholica semper in reformatione*. How often the Catholic Church has been described as the last relic left over from a bygone age, how often even declared to be dead —but it is precisely her periods of greatest decadence that have awoken in her again and again an unbroken will to reform. The history of the Catholic Church, with all the process of deformation that runs through it, is at the same time a history of a process of reformation, now secret, now public. While worldly kingdoms went down through decadence to death, the Catholic Church would fight her way up again to a new life; or, better, her living head, who is Christ, and her life-principle, who is the Holy Spirit, would reassert themselves in her once more.

A brief survey of the history of the Church as a history of renewal (with the Ecumenical Councils playing a decisive part in it) will help us to see the tasks of the coming Council in proper proportion. We do not propose to be comprehensive, but to point out certain important landmarks upon the way. Histories of the Church must be consulted for anything further.[1]

1. CATHOLIC RENEWAL BEFORE THE REFORMATION

This power of self-renewal is of course at work already in primitive Christianity. The apostolic Church itself was faced with problems of renewal and adaptation, and there has perhaps

[1] See, for example, J. Lortz, *Geschichte der Kirche in ideengeschichtlicher Betrachtung*, Münster, Westphalia, 1950; Bihlmeyer and Tüchle, *Kirchengeschichte*, 13th ed., Paderborn, 1952, vols. 1–3; Fliche and Martin, *Histoire de l'Eglise*, Paris, 1946–, vols. 1–24. For the history of the Popes: F. X. Seppelt, *Geschichte der Päpste*, 2nd ed., Munich, 1954, vols. 1–6; L. von Pastor, *History of the Popes*, London, 1891–1928 (vols. 1–16); J. Schmidlin, *Papstgeschichte der neuesten Zeit*, 2nd ed., Munich, 1933, vols. 1–4. For the history of the Councils: C. J. von Hefele, *Conciliengeschichte*, Freiburg im Breisgau, 1855–; 2nd ed., 1873–, vols. 1–9 (8 and 9 by Hergenröther); Leclercq, *Histoire des conciles d'après les documents originaux*, Paris, 1907–, vols 1–9; highly recommended for a brief factual survey: H. Jedin, *Ecumenical Councils in the Catholic Church: an Historical Survey* (London and Edinburgh, 1960); on the history of canon law: P. Hischius, *System des katholischen Kirchenrechts*, Berlin, 1883, vol. 3, of which pp. 325–473 are concerned with Ecumenical Councils.

never in the history of the Church been so
momentous an adaptation as that for which St.
Paul fought in his first mission to the Gentiles,
and which was authorized by the first Council
of the infant Church, the so-called Apostolic
Council of Jerusalem. It liberated the Church,
in practice, from the burden of the Jewish law,
overcame Jewish national preoccupations in the
Church, and opened the way for Christianity to
become a world religion.

One matter which was from the beginning a
constant subject of renewal was the liturgy,
which was far more susceptible of change and
adaptation in the first thousand years than it
has been in the second. The gigantic forward
thrust of the early Christian missions (un-
equalled by the missions of modern times,
though working with the most up-to-date techniques and with utter devotion) was based to a
great extent on the liturgy, which was constantly
adapted to new needs, and was celebrated in a
language which the people understood. There
was no rigid adherence to Aramaic or Hebrew
(respectively, the popular and liturgical languages of Palestine) but adaptation. So in Rome,
and in all the cultural and commercial centres
of the Roman Empire, the liturgy used the
koine Greek, which had, in the Hellenistic age,
replaced the local languages. But as soon as the
Gospel spread out from the great cities into the

hinterlands of Egypt, Syria or Armenia, the *koine* Greek was replaced by the corresponding local language. It is because of this period of steady adaptation that the Catholic Church today recognizes a whole series of official ecclesiastical and liturgical languages which were all then vernaculars: Western and Eastern Syriac (Aramaic), Greek, Coptic (Egyptian), Ethiopian, Armenian, Georgian, Gothic, Old Slavonic. There was a liturgical reform in Rome about the year 250: the original liturgical language of the Roman Christians was Greek (the oldest Roman eucharistic formulae, those of Justin and Hippolytus, were Greek); but because a different language was now being spoken by the people, the Greek was gradually replaced by Latin, the vernacular, which now became the liturgical language. Other adaptations followed in the Roman liturgy: the change from the celebration of Mass in the houses of the faithful, as in the third century, to celebration in the basilicas of the sixth to seventh centuries; and the transplanting, in the course of the eighth and ninth centuries, of the Roman liturgy (hitherto used only in Rome and its environs, and in the Anglo-Saxon missions) into France; but this time, no adaptation of language was attempted. From the tenth century onwards, the Frankish (Gallican) form of the Roman Mass was established even in Rome itself.

Another subject of constant renewal and adaptation, closely connected with the liturgy, was the translation of Scripture. As soon as the original biblical languages (Hebrew and Greek) were no longer understood by the people, the early Church set about producing translations for them: the various Greek and Aramaic translations of the Old Testament, and the Latin, Syriac, Coptic, Arabic, Ethiopian, Armenian, Georgian, Iranian, Gothic and Old Slavonic versions. There were constant reforms of the translations in any one language. There was the epoch-making task, given to St. Jerome by Pope Damasus I towards the end of the fourth century, of revising the entire Latin Bible. The revised translation was at first attacked as an "innovation", and was slow in gaining ground until the end of the eighth century; it then began to act as a barrier against translation into the vernacular (which was at this stage, in some cases, an unusable medium), and was finally dubbed the translation "in common use", or the Vulgate.

The self-renewing power of the Church then began to show itself especially in the Benedictine movement, in men like Benedict (note how the abuses among the itinerant monks were combated not by a negative but a positive solution —that monastic organization which was to set

the pattern for Western civilization), Cassio-
dorus and Gregory the Great (with special reference to pastoral work, the liturgy and the
missions). Then came the great work of adaptation in the German mission: first the Irish-
Scottish missions, embodying especially the reforming activity of Columbanus, in the sixth to
seventh centuries, then the reforming and organizing Anglo-Saxon mission under Boniface in
the eighth century, finally the planned reforms
of the Carolingian period, in ecclesiastical organization and education, in liturgy, preaching,
scholarship and pastoral work. Lastly, there is
the mission to the Slavs of SS. Cyril and
Methodius, which represents an even closer
approach to the people (Slavonic liturgy, etc.).

The eight Ecumenical Councils of the early
Church, which were all in the East, were primarily concerned with the definition of trini-
tarian and Christological dogma. But not
exclusively. For example, even the first of them,
that at Nicaea in 325, spent a month on the
discussion of practical questions (the reckoning
of the date of Easter, the treatment of those who
had lapsed under persecution, the ordination of
priests and bishops, the liturgy, the organization
of the Patriarchate of Alexandria, prohibition
of usury, etc.). The Fourth Ecumenical Council,
too, at Chalcedon in 451, had disciplinary questions to settle (the subordination of monks to

episcopal authority, the prohibition of ordinations without reference to any definite office, etc.).

After the collapse of the Carolingian Empire and Carolingian culture, the tenth century became a *saeculum obscurum* of the worst abuses in Church and Papacy. Renewal and reform had never been so necessary. The monasteries became the source of it. The centres of reform were in Lorraine (in the monasteries of Gorze and Brogne), in Italy (St. Nilus and St. Romauld, founder of the Camaldulenses), in Switzerland (Einsiedeln) and in England (Canterbury). But all were far outdone in influence by the Burgundian monastery of Cluny, whose rule finally extended over more than two thousand reforming monasteries throughout Europe.

Out of the Cluniac monastic reform of the eleventh century there quickly came a widespread reform of the clergy and finally a general reform of the Church. It was led by laymen: the German Emperors. The Ottonine Emperors had already made efforts, when they could, to reform the Papacy. But it was not till the reign of Henry III, a disciple of Cluny, who at the Synod of Sutri (1046) deposed three rival Popes and subsequently brought about the election of several good German Popes (elected, for the most part, at Councils of the Empire), that reform began to operate in Rome itself. It was the

Alsatian Pope, Leo IX (1049–54), who carried
it through. He travelled tirelessly, assembling
reforming synods, dedicating churches and
monasteries, fighting above all against the buy-
ing and selling of ecclesiastical office (simony)
and for the celibacy of the priesthood. With
Leo IX the leadership of reform passed from
the Emperors to the Popes, and the reforming
movement—in the shape of a battle of giants
between Empire and Papacy—reached its first
climax in that controversial figure but great
reformer Gregory VII (1073–85); but the emphasis had shifted from the strictly religious field to
that of ecclesiastical politics; to the matter
(which, indeed, often did involve simony) of lay
investiture, i.e., the endowment of clerics with
an abbey or bishopric by a secular ruler.

But the growth in the power of Church and
clergy had its inevitable negative consequences:
a worldly, ambitious and bureaucratic curia, and
worldly, because wealthy, monasteries. Against
this, new ascetic and reforming movements arose
in the shape of new *Orders*, in the strict sense;
not independent monasteries, but centrally
organized federations of monasteries. Following
after the Augustinian Canons, the Premonstra-
tensians and the Carthusians, this system was
effectively developed above all by the Cister-
cians. Here the reforming movement was led by
the most powerful mind of the twelfth century,

4*

Bernard of Clairvaux; criticism was levelled at
the wealth and power of established monastic-
ism (especially at Cluny) and emphasis laid on
simplicity and poverty (unadorned churches,
simple liturgy, work in the fields). The renewing effect of St. Bernard's work (even setting
aside the effect of his preaching on the Crusades)
extended throughout Europe. It was felt in an
interiorized and revitalized piety, wholly centred
upon Jesus in his earthly life (which connects
with the crusading ideal); it was felt in his Order,
spreading far afield from France; it was felt in
his influence on the highest authority in the
Church. A pupil of his was elected Pope as
Eugenius III (1145–53); ready as St. Bernard
was to praise the Papacy, he was no less ready
to criticize the Pope and the Romans, and not
to spare them even public rebuke.

The Church had grown rich and powerful.
This was worse than a persecution. It resulted
in abuses of every kind. Clearer and clearer, as
time went on, came the demand for reform,
often in the form of sects and popular movements; even in the eleventh century in the
religious-democratic movement of the Patarins
of Milan (to which Gregory VII gave his support in its struggle against the nobility and
higher clergy), in the democratic, strongly anti-
papal movement of Arnold of Brescia, and in

the Catharist and Waldensian sects (all condemned by the Church). These yearnings for
reform, often very deep-rooted and widespread,
their driving-power the ideal of poverty, were
taken up by the Church in the Mendicant
Orders; especially that of St. Francis of Assisi,
the flower of laymen, and also in the Dominicans, the Carmelites, the Augustinian Hermits,
and the Third Orders, chiefly associated with
the Franciscans and Dominicans, consisting of
lay associates carrying out the rule of their Order
in the world.

The work of St. Francis was approved by the
mightiest of all the medieval Popes, Innocent
III. It was he who, in 1215, summoned the
Fourth Lateran Council (the twelfth "Ecumenical") for the reform of the Church. The three
previous Councils of the Lateran, all recognized
as ecumenical by the Catholic Church, and all
continuing the tradition of Gregory VII's reforming movement, had already attended to
various problems of reform. Besides the Crusades and the Truce of God, they had made
rulings on simony, the appointment of bishops,
the election of the Pope, celibacy, plurality of
benefices, and various moral abuses. But the
Fourth Lateran Council surpassed all its predecessors, not only in splendour but in a reforming activity which, according to the Pope's plan

and intention, embraced every level of the Hierarchy and every degree in the Church. Its
seventy chapters, besides in part reaffirming
earlier decisions, deal with yearly confession and
Easter Communion as a minimum requirement;
the reduction of the number of impediments to
marriage, and the prohibition of clandestine
marriages; the prevention of fraud in pilgrimages and relics; the abuse of indulgences; improvement in the level of education in the
clergy; reverence in the recitation of the Breviary
and the celebration of Mass; provision for
preaching in the vernacular and for qualified
preachers and confessors; canon law concerning
the hearing of ecclesiastical causes; the shorten-
ing of the time during which a bishop's see could
remain vacant; yearly provincial synods, and
general chapters in the Orders, to supervise reform; and finally, the rectifying of various moral
abuses in clergy and laity.

But a year after the Council the Pope died,
and despite all these efforts no really fundamental renewal of the Church resulted from it.
Innocent III represents the high point in the
development of papal power in the Middle Ages,
and, at the same time, the beginning of its
decline. The triumph of the Papacy over the
Hohenstaufen Emperors proved to be a Pyrrhic
victory: the collapse of the *secular* pillar upon
which the arch of medieval order rested, the

decline of the universal imperial authority in the West and the resulting rise of democracy and nationalism, weakened the *spiritual* pillar, the universal papal authority. The Pope became dependent on France, this leading, in the fourteenth century, to the "exile" of the Popes in Avignon; then came the disastrous building up of the system of curial taxation, the encroachments of commercialization and nepotism in the Church's affairs, the whole leading to an almost unimaginable degradation of the Papacy. The end of Avignon was the Schism of the West, with three Popes, all excommunicating each other; an agony from which deliverance came only through another Ecumenical Council: Constance, 1414–18. But the final return of the Popes to Rome inaugurated the Renaissance Papacy; despite much good in the Church of that time, especially among the people, a rapid and catastrophic increase in worldliness set in, in head and members; there was an unprecedented decline in the morals of the Roman Curia, the bishops, the cathedral chapters, and the clergy; an appalling increase in proletariacy among the lower clergy; a decadent, turgid theology, often rating lower in men's minds than canon law; a discontent with the Church which was swiftly building up to frustration. The common battle-cry of the best spirits, whether sorrowful or impatient or enraged, was

"Reform!". *Gravamina*—lists of grievances—
and proposals for reform multiplied without
end.

Even this dismal autumn of the Middle Ages
was not without its attempts at renewal. There
had been religious revolutionaries who had condemned the Church's leaders: in Italy (after
Joachim of Fiore, a man far ahead of his time)
there was Marsiglio of Padua, in England John
Wiclif, and in Bohemia the latter's follower
John Hus; in these men, just criticism and valid
religious aspirations had mingled with the
widest variety of democratic tendencies, nation-
alist and toward the school of the "spirituals".
But there were other reformers and reforming
circles who were loyally devoted to the Church;
a large number of the humanists, for instance;
in Holland, the Brothers of the Common Life
and, originating from them, the reformed congregation of the Augustinian Canons (among
their pupils were Nicholas of Cusa, Erasmus of
Rotterdam, the author of the *Imitation of Christ*,
and the reforming Pope Adrian VI); in Spain,
the great reformer Cardinal Ximenes; then
there were the Observants in the various Orders,
and the numerous preachers of penance (Vincent Ferrer, Bernardine of Siena, John Capi-
stran, Geronimo Savonarola). But none of them,
despite the genuine popular piety which they
had to work on, and despite the movement of

German mysticism, had any really far-reaching success.

All the *official* attempts at reforming the Church in these centuries dwindled equally into despair. The papal oath to carry out a reform, taken at the beginning of each Renaissance pontificate, was as ineffectual as the series of Ecumenical Councils to achieve any genuine renewal. These Councils failed because, for many different reasons, they did not embark boldly on any radical reform but stuck fast on superficialities.

The two Ecumenical Councils after the four Councils of the Lateran took place in Lyons. At the first of these, under Innocent IV (1245), apart from a reorganization of canon law, the main object was not so much reform of the Church as the deposition of the Hohenstaufen Emperor Frederick II. The second, under Gregory X (1274), was dominated by the Turkish perils, called for a new Crusade and led to a union with the Greek Church (the former Patriarch of Constantinople and the Chancellor of the Byzantine Emperor took part in the Council); the reunion, being motivated chiefly by political considerations, did not last. Reform of the Church came in only for a few decrees on the papal election (the introduction of the conclave), on elections of bishops, and on the bishops' complaints against the privileges of the

Mendicant Orders. The fifteenth Ecumenical Council, that of Vienne (1311–12), under the first of the Avignon Popes, Clement V, had as the third of its objects (together with the suppression of the Order of the Temple and the settling of the Franciscan dispute over poverty) the matter of Church reform. The far-seeing proposals of Durandus of Mende, to which reference has already been made, were not adopted. Instead of discussing his suggestions for limiting, in practice, the area of direct papal administration, or his plans for strengthening the power of the bishops, for reviving the ancient system of Church synods, and for raising the level of education among the clergy, the Council spoke only of secular encroachments in the sphere of the Church's courts, taxes and finances, and of administrative hindrances suffered by the bishops on account of the innumerable papal dispensations and other privileges.

The sixteenth Ecumenical Council, Constance (1414–18), had to devote all its energies to ending the Western Schism. Once the new Pope was elected, there was no unanimity about what shape reform (more and more urgently needed as it was) should take. Some limitations were introduced on the scope of papal interference, but nothing was done amounting to genuine reform. The following period was marked by the struggle of the Papacy against the strong Conciliarist movement, which placed the Council above the Pope. The Council which began at Basle in 1431 did indeed make a start on Church reform (with promising decrees on liturgy, on needless appeals of cases to Rome, and on the regular holding of provincial and diocesan synods), but it was Conciliarist in character, and was transferred by Eugene IV first to Ferrara (1437) and finally to Florence (1439). Here it achieved but again on predominantly political grounds—a union with the Greeks, the Armenians and the monophysite Jacobites, which again did not last.

It still seemed that Church reform would be possible only through an Ecumenical Council. But the Renaissance Popes wanted neither a Council nor any serious reform. However, an anti-papal "council" at Pisa compelled Julius II to summon an Ecumenical Council at Rome. Once more, at this Fifth Lateran Council (the eighteenth "ecumenical"), held from 1512 to 1517, the spokesmen of radical reform (such as the Camaldulenses Giustiniani and Quirini) were unable to make their voices prevail; a few meagre reforming decrees were passed (on curial taxation, election of bishops, religious instruction and preaching, etc.), but there was no prospect of their being effectively carried out by those responsible. Still, even at this Council protestations of the necessity for reform were being made on all sides.

Six months after the close of the Council, reform had come with a vengeance: Luther's theses and the Reformation.

We must now face the disturbing question, which can neither be answered in a few sentences nor simply avoided:

2. WHY DID THE CATHOLIC CHURCH REJECT THE PROTESTANT REFORM?

We are not going to try to make a critical examination of all the complex causes, conditions and factors of the Reformation movement that started from Luther, tracing them back into the early Middle Ages, above ground and below, through all the developments of thought and culture, philosophy and theology, ecclesiastical and religious life, Church–State relations and all. Nor shall we make a critical assessment of the complicated and problematical genesis of Martin Luther the Reformer, nor of the development in Germany and Europe generally of the Reformation in its Lutheran, Anglican, Calvinist and Baptist-Independent forms. It is a hopeful omen for reunion that the latest presentations of Church history from both sides, on the subject of the Reformation and its causes, bear a strong resemblance to each other.[1] Both sides nowadays see the good in the other and the evil in their

[1] The standard Catholic work today is that of J. Lortz, *Die Reformation in Deutschland*, Freiburg im Breisgau, 1948, 2 vols.

own. Protestant criticism of the formerly almost sacrosanct character of Luther and of the reform which he instituted is nowadays as little out of the ordinary as Catholic recognition of the positive religious aspirations of Luther and the Reformation. Protestants see the positive values in the Church of that age, and Catholics recognize the Church's share in the guilt of schism. This confession of guilt on the Catholic side is by no means new. At the time of the Reformation itself Pope Adrian VI made the famous confession of guilt at the Diet of Ratisbon (1522–23), and so did many leading Catholics of that time, as for example the Papal Legate Cardinal Contarini, Cardinal Pole, who presided at the Council of Trent, and the commission of cardinals who produced, for Paul III, that famous programme of reform, *De Emendanda Ecclesia*; these are followed by St. Peter Canisius, St. Clement Hofbauer, Cardinal Newman, and many others down to Pius XI. The list includes the present Pope John XXIII, when, with direct reference to the coming Ecumenical Council, he said in an address to the clergy of his diocese, "We do not wish to put anyone in history on trial; we shall not seek to establish who was right and who was wrong. Responsibility is divided. We only want to say: Let us come together, let us make an end of our divisions."[1]

[1] *Herder-Korrespondenz*, (1959–60), pp. 274 f.

We only aim here, without laying any further foundation, to state briefly why the Catholic Church rejected the Reformation of Luther and the Reformers. Any Catholic answer would have to bear the following elements in mind:

(1) Because of the whole intellectual, theological, religious and moral situation at the time, neither Rome nor the Church's leaders elsewhere were, for the most part, in a fit state to understand the spiritual needs of the age in all their profundity; nor, hence, to grasp Luther's theological and practical demands and give a convincing answer, on a Catholic basis, to the questions that arose; new questions called, of necessity, for new answers. To understand the theological demands, what was needed, and was sadly lacking in that age when theology had grown unsure of itself, was a theology in which important key-points had been profoundly and clearly thought out, which was concentrated upon essentials, and which was primarily focused upon the Scriptures (and this in the minds not only of theologians but of those in pastoral office). To understand the practical demands, what was sadly lacking was clear-sightedness (it was not realized that abuses were to a great extent rooted in false structural accretions), self-critical humility, the moral energy and effective will to improve, interest in religious matters, and any effort to live according to the example of Christ.

(2) Luther, on his side, for a variety of personal and psychological as well as theological, religious and historical reasons was incapable of grasping the true form of Catholicism behind its deformity. Because of his misunderstanding of the nature of the Catholic Church, which was indeed at that time badly obscured and deformed, much of what he rejected as essential to the Catholic Church was in fact thoroughly uncatholic (e.g., in nominalist theology, in the popular piety and liturgy of his day, and in the condition of the Hierarchy). On the other hand, he believed that many of his own demands, which were, as time was to show, basically entirely Catholic, were quite incompatible with the Catholic Church against which he was fighting. A whole series of Luther's motives for leaving the Catholic Church did, in this sense, rest on misunderstandings.

Is our schism, then, a pure misunderstanding on both sides? No; for two other elements must be considered before we can understand why the Catholic Church rejected Luther's Reformation:

(3) Despite Luther's good intentions—and again for a variety of reasons arising out of the whole bedevilled situation, his own psychological and religious temperament, and his upbringing, education and experience—he took certain perfectly Catholic principles and in some cases

formulated them so as to give the maximum risk
of misunderstanding, disunity and sheer contradiction, and in others asserted them with a onesided stress which was not only polemical but
actually heretical. Even Protestant theologians
admit today that Luther (and hence the other
Reformers too) did not have St. Paul and the
Scriptures behind them in all their declarations
and demands, and were to this extent mistaken
in particular points of their understanding of
the Faith. Even those who see much that is
positive in them cannot simply regard Luther
and the Reformers as perfect hearers of the
Word of God. In this sense, they *had* to be
rejected by the Catholic Church.

(4) The actual reason for rejecting Luther
was this: For all that it included genuine reforms, and despite his conservatism, often
stressed today, Luther's Reformation was essentially a revolution. He brought the very essence
of the Catholic Church into question when (this
was the real innovation) he set his personal,
subjective, and yet (by his intention) universally
binding interpretation of the Scriptures *in
principle* above the Church and her tradition.
This meant that he rejected the whole teaching
office of the Church, not only in the Pope but,
after the Leipzig Disputation in 1519, in the
Ecumenical Councils as well. St. Francis of
Assisi, fighting his similar battle for the pure

Gospel, had faced similar difficulties to Luther's; but, in his oneness with the Church, he found a different solution. Catholics can have the greatest respect for the human and religious genius of Luther, but they have great difficulty in seeing him as a saint and reformer on the scale of St. Francis. Nor can it be denied that the Reformation did not bring, as Luther expected, a restoration of the Church on the pattern of primitive Christianity. On the contrary, the history of the process of subdivision in Protestantism and its dialectical transformations into the different varieties of modern Protestantism have, in our eyes, justified the Church authorities of that age.

Who could fail to see a mass of ambiguity in all this, thus briefly stated? We have no intention of self-righteously settling the problem of the Reformation as a whole in these brief notes, for they are no more. To return to the Pope's words, we have no wish to put anyone in history on trial. No, not Luther himself, who did originally desire a reform *within* the Church; who to some extent, because of the forced situation in which he was historically placed, grew away from the Church; and who could justly ask any Catholic who thinks that he can summarily judge his "case", what, in that forced situation, he ought to have done. Responsibility is divided, says the Pope. We have made these points only to shed a little light on the grave reasons why the Catholic Church rejected Luther and the Protestant Reformation in general and why, if she was not prepared to surrender her very nature, she was bound to do so.

But—must it forever remain so? Are protest and counter-protest to be the last and final word?

3. CATHOLIC RESTORATION OR CATHOLIC RENEWAL?

A protest, even though justified in its time, should not necessarily be repeated forever. Do Protestant preachers and theologians give enough thought to this? We do not maintain that there has been no proper matter for protest. But the protest needs re-examining; for the Catholic Church has not been standing still. She did indeed reject the Protestant Reformation, but she did not reject reform. She did not choose to become a "Reformed Church", but she has not therefore remained an unreformed Church. Catholic renewal is a fact. We do not exactly pride ourselves on it; men had been clamouring for it for centuries, but, to our shame and remorse, it was only *after* Luther had struck his blow and it had become unavoidable that it was actually done.

Both the Reformation and the Counter-Reformation had their political aspects. But it

would be wrong in either case to regard the
political aspect as primary. At the root of the
Reformation, and of the—somewhat misnamed
—Counter-Reformation too, there lay a strictly
religious need, the need for reform, for a renewal
of the Church in accordance with her true
nature. Reform within the Catholic Church was
first aroused and afterwards kept awake by
Luther's thunderbolt: to this extent it was a
Counter-Reformation. But it was not only that.[1]
If we look at what it was in the concrete, we find
that its driving power came, in the first place,
not from forces connected with the Reformers
but from reforming impulses dating from before
the Reformation. We have already, in a previous
section, indicated some of these forces: reforming preachers, reformers of individual Orders,
reforming impulses in particular bishops and in
particular groups with an enthusiastic interest
in reform, the world of classical scholarship, the
devotio moderna, the mystical movement. The
renewal, when it came, made use of all these
pre-Reformation forces. Indeed, in its basic aims
and programme, it was already in existence, but

[1] Cf. H. Jedin, *Katholische Reformation oder Gegen-
reformation?*, Lucerne, 1946; and R. G. Villoslada, S.J.,
"La Contrareforma. Su nombre y su concepto historico",
in *Saggi Storici intorno al Papato dei Professori della
Facoltà di Storia Ecclesiastica*, Pont. Univ. Gregoriana,
Rome, 1959, *Miscellanea Historiae Pontificiae*, vol. 21,
pp. 189–242.

while it remained simply a reform of the Body's members by themselves, it could develop only very slowly and amid numerous hindrances and set-backs. Catholic reform did not come out of the lands of the Reformation; it was outside that area, in Italy and afterwards in Spain, that these authentically Catholic forces were aroused. From this time forward the Catholic Church displays a markedly Roman character.

The foundations of Catholic reform (apart from reform of the Orders) were laid in small and apparently insignificant things: in the brotherhoods and oratories in Italy, like the Roman Oratory of the Divine Love, where clergy and laity together cultivated a deep humanistic piety. It produced Gaetano of Thiene's Theatine Order for the reform of the clergy, and a future reforming Pope, Caraffa. There was another group of reformers in Venice round Gasparo Contarini. But it was not till the Sack of Rome when imperial troops devastated Renaissance Rome in 1527, that reform found room to breathe and grow. Adrian VI had died too soon to achieve anything. It was Paul III (1534–49) who made reform the official concern of the Papacy itself. Though himself deeply imbued with the spirit of the Renaissance, his were the decisive acts which brought reform to Rome; he appointed to the College of Cardinals men (including laymen!) who were at once extremely able and deeply religious: Contarini, Pole, Fisher of Rochester, Morone, Caraffa; and men of this group compiled for the Pope the famous report on the state of the Church, *De Ememdenda Ecclesia*. He gave approval to the foremost of the Counter-Reformation Orders, the Society of Jesus. And finally, in 1545, he opened the Council of Trent.

The Council of Trent, so long awaited, so constantly postponed by the Popes, was the nineteenth Ecumenical Council.[1] It dealt, to some extent in parallel fashion, both with the affirmation of dogma and with the working out of practical reforms. Its achievements in both spheres were notable. Its doctrinal decrees treat of the sources of faith, original sin, justification, the sacraments, the sacrifice of the Mass. Its disciplinary decrees concern marriage, the education of the clergy and the erection of diocesan seminaries, the bishops' duties of residence and visitation, prohibition of holding a plurality of sees and benefices, the nomination and duties of bishops and cardinals, the holding of annual diocesan synods and triennial provincial synods, the reform of cathedral chapters and religious Orders, etc. The Council of Trent became an

[1] See the Acts of the Council (*Editio Goerresiana*) and the standard modern Catholic work, H. Jedin, *A History of the Council of Trent,* trans. Graf, London and Edinburgh, Nelson, 1957–61, 2 vols.

epoch-making, universal expression of the
Church's reform of herself from within, rooted
in the central core of Catholicism.

In the sphere of doctrine, the purpose of
Trent was to define Catholic teaching against
that of the Reformers. But even here one must
not overlook the element of positive interior
reform accompanying the anti-Protestant, and
especially anti-Lutheran element. It is far more
significant than is generally realized that the
really fundamental dogmatic definitions were
drawn up during the first period of the Council,
1545–7. Formally, they are strongly character-
ized by abstention from scholastic disputes and
by the effort, largely successful, to express Catholic doctrine in Biblical language. The decree on
justification, which is the glory of the Council,
accepts what is valid in the Reformers' position
to a surprising degree.

Nor was the Council's work of reform in the
narrower sense merely a Counter-Reformation.
We have to think of the new forms brought into
being in the education of priests, in the life of
religious Orders, in preaching, religious practices, culture, art, mysticism; of the organizing
of pastoral and catechetical work, of the missions,
of the care of the poor and the sick. Finally, we
have to think of the religious renewal in Italy,
Spain and France in the sixteenth and seven-
teenth centuries, and of the great figures of that

period: the Jesuit founder Ignatius of Loyola, the Carmelite reformer Teresa of Avila, the founder of the Oratorians, Philip Neri; then, quite as significant in their very different ways, the reformers of the Curia, such as Pius V and Charles Borromeo; Cardinal Fisher and the English martyrs; the Jesuits Peter Canisius, Robert Bellarmine, Francis Borgia, Aloysius Gonzaga, Stanislaus Kostka; the Spanish mystics and reformers John of the Cross, John of God and Peter of Alcántara; the great Frenchmen Francis of Sales, Vincent de Paul, Bérulle, Fénelon, Bourdaloue, Massillon, Pascal; and in the realm of ecclesiastical scholarship, Petavius, the Maurists, the Bollandists . . . a sequence of famous names, each standing for a multitude of less famous ones. All this was no mere restoration of the Middle Ages but, in the best sense, a reform, a renewal.

But all this is only one side of that period of Catholic reform. Side by side with Catholic reform as a positive inner renewal stands Catholic reform as a fight against Protestantism, a *Counter*-Reformation, stamped all over with the character of *restoration*. Reform, yes, of course; for the dangers threatening an unreformed Church are now recognized; it is only possible to confront Protestantism if one has reformed oneself. The spread of Protestantism must be checked, lost territory reconquered and missionary territory in the newly-discovered continents conquered in addition. This means, then, not really trying to understand Protestant demands positively, from within, and then to carry them out oneself so far as they are justified, so as to go as far as possible to meet Protestantism, lovingly and repentantly. It means trying, by a reform of Catholicism, to *combat* Protestantism; it means reform within the Church not as a means to reconciliation and reunion but as an armaments programme and a plan of campaign. Hence we see much of the Catholic reform of that time displaying itself as *reaction,* in the sense of a restoration aimed at maintaining what was established and restoring according to the pattern of a superior past, with the consequent danger of stunting and fossilizing the fullness of Catholicism. The liturgy, both in the Mass and the Divine Office, is not re-formed, creatively, through a deep understanding of the Reformers' demands, but simply "restored to its former purity"; and the pattern is not primarily that of the liturgy as described in the Scriptures or practised in the early Church, but that of the Middle Ages. In theology, too, those forces of which we have already spoken, which were at work in the first period of the Council, were not sufficiently effective in the long run (though their effect, as embodied in the decrees, could never be lost, and is beginning today to bear fruit). The effort made was often not to think things out afresh, from their original source in the Scriptures, with reference to the new age and its needs, and to restate them boldly and creatively, accepting what was valid in the Reformers' challenge. It was rather to maintain, defensively, "purity of doctrine". Similarly, in pastoral work and the conduct of the Church's affairs, it is often simply the expedient of "maintaining traditional practice" that comes to the fore. It is impossible to overlook a dangerous hardening in all this from the time of Paul IV and his manner of conducting the Inquisition. In the missions, too, the ideal was not so much a general adaptation and entry of the Church into the individualities of different peoples, in their religious speech, their religious thought, their religious customs, but rather a strongly centralized "conquest for the Kingdom of Christ"; here indeed we have one of the most disastrous weaknesses in the post-Reformation life of the Church. From the first century until well into the Middle Ages, the Church's missionary practice had been patterned according to the rule of prudent accommodation to local custom; the setting aside of this rule (in the Chinese Rites dispute), despite all the enormous sacrifices and marvellous achievements of missionaries, laid the foundation for that failure in the missionary work of recent centuries of which we are becoming aware today.

Thus the position was reached in which the Church was confronting Protestantism in an irreconcilable opposition, and the unlovely accompaniments of this type of restoration-reform are all too familiar to us: negative polemics, narrowmindedness, violent elimination of abuses and defence of the purity of doctrine by inquisitorial methods; political denominational manœuvrings in the secular sphere; and, worst of all, "religious" wars. The fact that we can match each of these items from the record of anti-Catholic Protestantism is no consolation to us.

But what even Catholics are largely unaware of is this: that at the time of the beginnings of Catholic reform, under Paul III, "Renewal or restoration?" was a thoroughly real question. There was a strong current in the highest circles in the Church making for positive renewal; men who had a positive approach to many of the Reformers' demands, who were ready and willing for discussion and therefore tended ultimately towards some kind of accommodation with Protestantism.[1] There had, of course, to be a certain process of argument with Protestantism too (even apart from those areas of direct

[1] Cf. a historical study by J. Fischer, shortly to be published, on the different concepts of reform in Cardinal Reginald Pole on the one hand and Gian Pietro Caraffa on the other.

contact with it in North and South Italy which were centres of irritation). But in the main these were arguments about problems arising out of the Bible, especially St. Paul, and having their effect throughout Europe on groups of men concerned with the meaning of the Gospel: problems about justification, the *theologia crucis,* the invisible Church, etc.—concerned, in fact, with the same points as those which were central to the Reformation. In men like Scripando, foremost of all in this matter, Contarini and Pole, the mental stimulus came not from the Reformation movement but simply from the Bible. This was a movement within the Catholic Church, closely related to the religious aspirations of the Reformation (though not to its theological formulae) but all within an emphatic adherence to the sacramental and hierarchical Church. Besides the Viterbo circle (with Michelangelo and Vittoria Colonna) and the two Camaldulenses Quirini and Giustiniani (who had presented their bold recommendations for reform to Leo X), the chief members of this group were Cardinals Contarini, Sadoleto, Cervini, Pole, Morone and Seripando, who were in communication with German humanists, German Catholic theologians such as Pighius, Gropper and Pflug, and leaders in political affairs, especially in the Emperor's entourage. It was cardinals of this group who had produced

the *De Emendanda Ecclesia*. Their leader was
Contarini, who, as Papal Legate, tried to reach
a reconciliation with the Lutherans at the Diet
of Ratisbon (1541) with his, admittedly inadequate, doctrine of "double justification". But
it was not this group which prevailed. Contarini
was suspected of heresy and died the following
year. The same year saw the foundation of the
central Roman Inquisition (Sacrum Officium
Sanctissimae Inquisitionis), under that exponent
of reform as a conservative restoration, Cardinal
Gian Pietro Caraffa, who also produced the first
edition of the Index. And again in the same
year, the famous Capuchin preacher and reformer Bernardino Occhino fled to Calvin, and
with him some of the most passionate champions
of renewal deserted the cause and fell, in despair,
into the extremes of heresy (to the point of
antitrinitarianism, etc.). Others were imperilled
and compelled to be silent. Nevertheless, until
the death of Paul III the Roman Inquisition was
extraordinarily moderate in its proceedings. The
question of what direction reform should take
was, in its main lines, settled in favour of restoration when Caraffa was elected Pope in 1555.

Nor was there any spirit of reconciliation on
the Protestant side. Denominational frontiers
hardened; the two groups of separated brethren,
unwilling even to recognize each other now,
began to devote themselves entirely to mutual

strife, and so to grow away from each other in every respect and to fall into a total estrangement. Caraffa's great successors, after his ruinous excursions into secular and family politics, the reforming Popes Pius V, Gregory XIII, Sixtus V and so on, all belonged not to the Contarini group but to the party of restoration. The work went on with intense energy: restoration of the Vulgate (Vulgata Sixto-Clementina), restoration of the liturgy, both of the Latin Mass, regulated now down to the smallest detail (pruned of a mass of excrescences, but without any approach to the liturgical needs of the people) and of the Latin Breviary. The excellent reformed Breviary designed, at Clement VII's suggestion, by the Spanish Cardinal Quiñones for private recitation, had been enthusiastically adopted under Paul III. The rubrics were extremely simple; everything arising directly from the practice of choral recitation (versicles, antiphons, chapters) was eliminated; the whole of the New Testament and the greater part of the Old were read in the course of a year, and the psalms were reduced to three for each Hour. This Breviary ran through a hundred editions in a few years; but in 1558 it was forbidden by Paul IV, and in 1568 Pius V published, and made obligatory, a restored Breviary in the traditional form.

Further restoration was carried out on the Curia (reorganization and, in part, creation of the Roman Congregations, and erection of permanent nunciatures) and on the religious Orders. All this was accompanied by the issuing of the Roman Catechism, the introduction of book censorship, and the activities of the Inquisition and the Congregation of the Index. It hardly needs stressing here that, for all their limitations, these acts of restoration were productive of immeasurable good. It is thanks to them that the Church of the Baroque period displays a purity and strength very different from the Church of the Renaissance.

During this same period there was a strengthening of papal authority, leading to a growing centralization in the government and teaching office of the Church; a development culminating in the Vatican Council with its definition of the primacy and infallibility of the Pope. But this strengthening of papal authority was stringently necessary, for the Church was passing through stormy times. Each wave of attack was succeeded by another. Lutheranism and Calvinism were followed by Jansenism, Gallicanism, royal absolutism, the Enlightenment, Febronianism and then, with the dawn of a new age, the French Revolution, secularization, the Napoleonic wars, atheistic materialism, liberalism and socialism. Bound up with all this, in the eighteenth century in particular, there came a decline in the Church. She was faced with a multitude of new problems, new questions, new needs. Masses of people were falling away from the Church, both among the educated classes and in the new proletariat. Rejection of the Church had passed on to rejection of Christ and finally of God himself. The need was all the greater for the faithful to close their ranks in defence. There was a really grave danger of the Church's falling apart (as the history of Protestantism in these centuries shows) and a correspondingly urgent need to rally to the centre: against foes outside the Church and heretics within (Baius, Jansen, the Quietists, the Rationalists, the Fideists); against all-powerful states; against the swift succession of popular and philosophical revolutions.

The Church had her great achievements, even in the much-despised nineteenth century. We need only think of her lying prostrate at the beginning of that century: Pius VI dying, a prisoner, at Valence in 1799; Pius VII again Napoleon's prisoner; in France, now the ruler of Europe, the Church pronounced dead, large numbers of her priests killed or banished, her Orders weakened or abolished, her organization smashed, her temporal goods and schools lost to her, religious life at its lowest ebb. But then, in this very century, comes an undreamt-of flowering of the Church's life and an interiorization of religion. There are developments in catechetical and pastoral work, with reference to various conditions of life; new specialized Congregations; new associations and forms of devotion; new impulses in the missions, especially through lay participation in the missionary movement. Great things were achieved in the period of post-Napoleonic restoration and in the Catholic Romantic movement; then again on the part of the Orders (Jesuits and Redemptorists in particular), and finally by men like St. Clement Hofbauer, Sailer, Hirscher and the Catholic theologians of the Tübingen School (such as J. A. Möhler and F. Staudenmeier) in Germany; Chateaubriand, De Maistre, De Lamennais and Lacordaire in France; and by such outstanding figures as the apostle of charity, Frederick Ozanam, founder of the Society of St. Vincent de Paul; John Bosco, apostle of youth; Thérèse of Lisieux; and Cardinal Newman.

Yet most of what happened in the Church during this period bore heavy traces of being primarily a defensive, rearguard action against the overpowering assaults of the spirit of the age. It was realized all too little in the nineteenth-century Church that even revolutions become normal in time, that they have their positive, permanent kernel, and that the Church stands not only to lose but also, as the future was to show, to gain from them.

It seemed from outside as though the Catholic Church were against not only what was false and pernicious in modern movements but also against the *goodness* and *truth* that they contained: as though she were against even what was *true* in modern philosophy, literature and science; against even what was *good* in democracy (especially in France, where the one line of cleavage between men was their judgement of the great Revolution) and in the national movements (especially Italy's struggle for national liberty); against even the *valid* aspirations in liberalism (civil toleration and liberty) and in socialism (radical reconstruction of the social order), and so forth. Ultimately, this was not the case, as the sequel was to show. But it is impossible to deny that there was much that seemed to indicate it.

As for Protestantism, the hot war against it was followed by a period in which it was coldly ignored. Catholics were as unaware as Protestants that it was, more and more, the basis common to both of them that was being threatened. Apart from some moves towards understanding at the beginning of the nineteenth century, on the part of Gallitzin and Sailer, sheer antagonism to Protestantism caused an almost total blindness to the wound made by schism and for the Catholic share in responsibility for it. At the same time the Church's (as it seemed from outside) anti-modern attitude provoked an anti-clericalism which drew nourishment from many sources and was often furious in its intensity. It got to the point of what was in Germany called the *Kulturkampf*. Not the least of the barriers against taking a more positive attitude towards the modern world was the Papal State. The concrete situation there constantly and inevitably showed the Popes in an anti-national, anti-democratic, anti-lay, anti-social, anti-liberal light; its load of social abuses (despite attempts at reform), its administrative deficiencies, the repression of criticism within it, and the interventions of foreign powers were all a heavy drag on the Papacy.

There is furthermore much that is ambivalent (as is indeed always the case in history) in the manifest religious revival of the nineteenth century. It suffered from off-centredness, a frequent displacement of emphasis onto the peripheral things of the Faith. Liturgical piety was forced, during the nineteenth century, to give place to innumerable devotions and votive feasts. Too little account was taken of the Scriptures; the practice of reading the Epistle and Gospel of the Mass from the pulpit declined, as did the preaching of sermons closely related to, and explaining, the Scriptures; the fight against the Protestant Bible Societies led all too often to a restriction of Bible reading among Catholics themselves. Both in theology and in the Church's art original impulses were, on the whole, lacking; there was no attempt to reach an understanding from the inside of contemporary currents of thought: everything was a looking-backwards, a restoration of the past (neo-Gothic, neo-Romanesque, etc.). There were numerous condemnations of the errors of the age by the teaching voice of the Church; so numerous, that Pius IX gathered them together into a single long Syllabus (*Collectio Errorum Modernorum*), generally regarded as a total rejection by the Catholic Church of modern culture and progress. Of course we are aware that this survey stresses only one line in the Church's development; it cannot cover the whole. The positive side of religion (often out of sight, but nevertheless deeply rooted) was important in this century too. But this does not cancel out the deficiencies we have instanced; it did not alter the Church's onesided, defensive attitude towards everything in the modern world.

The exigencies of defensive warfare gave Pius IX the idea of summoning a new Ecumenical Council, so as "by this exceptional means to help the Church out of her exceptional difficulties" (according to the first communication of the plan to the Cardinals on 6 Dec. 1864); so as "to find the necessary means of salvation against the evils, alas so numerous, which oppress the

5*

Church" (according to the public proclamation of the Council on 26 June 1867). On 8 Dec. 1869 the Vatican Council, the twentieth "ecumenical", was opened.[1] Apart from the definitions of the primacy and the infallibility of the Pope, already referred to, which were again products of the pressing needs of the times, the Council's chief concern was with affirmations against the errors of the day; the decree on faith was aimed chiefly at materialism, deism and the various forms of pantheism; at fideism, traditionalism and rationalism; and against the Güntherians and Hermesians. Expectations of practical reform were not fulfilled. Proposals for reform were indeed presented, three hundred columns in folio of them. But the bishops did not, as a whole, approve of the schemata that had been prepared. Their demands were for reforming legislation on the Curia, the Congregations and the College of Cardinals (especially an equitable division of the membership of the latter according to the size and importance of different nations in the Church); for a definition not only of the duties but above all of the rights

[1] On the history of the Vatican Council, cf. Mansi and the *Collectio Lacensis* for the documents; T. Granderath, *Geschichte des Vatikanischen Konzils*, Freiburg im Breisgau, 1903–, vols. 1–3; Butler, *The Vatican Council*, London, 1930; R. Aubert, *Le Pontificat de Pie IX*, Paris, 1952, in Fliche and Martin, *Histoire de l'Église*, vol. 21.

of bishops (decentralization, reduction in number of matters reserved to Rome, increase of those within the full power of the bishop, etc.); reform of the Breviary; better adaptation to the conditions of the time; concentration on the main lines of reform rather than on a mass of details, etc. But in spite of discussions lasting from January 8th to February 22nd, of the re-drafting of the decrees, and of fresh discussions in May, none of the schemata ever came to the point of publication. And the results of the labours of the third and fourth commissions (the first and second being those on faith and discipline), on the religious Orders, the Oriental Churches and the missions, were never even debated. Forty-six schemata were prepared on discipline and on the life of the Orders; four were discussed; not one was approved. The assembly, almost eight hundred strong, made an unwieldy vehicle for discussion, and the whole debate finally became concentrated on the questions of primacy and infallibility. The definition was made on the 18 July 1870. The following day the Franco-Prussian War broke out; the Council had to be adjourned; to this day it has never been formally concluded. On the 21 Sept. Rome was stormed by the Italians. It was the end of a thousand years of papal secular sovereignty.

A new age began for the Church and the

Papacy. It cannot simply be separated from what ment before; innumerable lines of continuity were preserved. But there is a plainly visible turning-point, not only in the loss of the Papal State and the various external convulsions, but even more in what followed the papal election of 1878. The man of the new era was Leo XIII. The Church of the preceding period had been built like a fortress; each of the manifold attacks and inroads made on her had brought about— though with heavy losses in territory and troops —a further closing of the ranks, a further withdrawal towards the centre; there had to be increased centralization to withstand the storm. Those outside could look only with dislike and suspicion on this grim, inhospitable fortress, wholly organized for defence, for repelling attack, for counter-attack, where every bastion seemed to be manned and every drawbridge raised as though in perpetual state of emergency. It was an eyesore, an erection of the *ancien régime* and reactionary obscurantism, ripe for destruction. It was to be hoped that, shut in on itself as it was, it would soon suffocate. But the event proved otherwise.

Excelling his predecessors in flexibility of mind and by his sober readiness to meet others half-way; freed, willy-nilly, from the burden (no longer a support) of the Papal State; equipped with a clearly-defined and at the same time spiritualized authority, and able to count on an

increased solidarity among his followers and to
make use of his predecessor's clear lines of de-
marcation in respect of modern thought, Leo
XIII certainly did not demolish the fortress, but
he threw open its gates and its windows, even in
his very first encyclical. And the effect did not
fail to follow. Individual measures, which may
well be of disputable value in themselves, are
less important than the fact that the whole
atmosphere changed; fresh air blew through the
Church, and men breathed more freely. One
symbol of the change came in the very first year
of the new pontificate: a simple priest, John
Henry Newman, an object of violent enmity and
suspicion to Catholics of the integralist type, was
made a cardinal of the Roman Church. Without
any conscious connection with the more eirenic
group in the Reformation Curia, but in a way
that was spiritually akin to it, a definite, fresh
beginning was made under Leo XIII on a reform
of the Church which was not merely a conservative restoration but a positive, creative renewal.
Amongst those sixteenth-century cardinals, how
much more like was Leo, in his character and
his whole relationship to the Church and the
world, to Contarini and Pole than to the future
Popes Caraffa and Ghislieri! Again, in contrast
to his predecessors Gregory XVI and Pius IX,
Leo XIII had a fundamentally positive relationship to that modern world which had been growing up in the meanwhile. In his view, the

Church ought not simply to resist, to condemn, to deny, but, while making no compromise in essentials, to assent, to assist and to co-operate so as to win the modern world by achieving a genuine relationship with the new age.

And this was no mere declaration of intention but was demonstrated in what Leo actually did. We must not fix our eyes here on all that is still missing, but rather on what is, in comparison with the preceding period, so marvellously new.

Leo devoted himself, successfully, to ending the *Kulturkampf* in Germany, and to improving relations with the modern states generally, which had steadily deteriorated under Pius IX. He gave support in his encyclicals to the political framework of the modern state (even in the field of Church-State relations) and compelled the Restoration-fixated French Catholics to come to terms with French democracy. He grappled in a positive way with the modern problem of liberty (in *Libertas Praestantissimum*), and, admitting what was valid in the aims of liberalism and socialism, proposed a positive and constructive solution to the social question (*Rerum Novarum*).

He called for a re-founding of scholarship within the Church, in archaeology, in theology (neo-Thomism being by no means, in the long view taken by the Pope, a mere restoration) and in exegesis (with the foundation of the Biblical

Commission, intended to promote high standards of scholarship and theological exactitude in biblical studies, with the plan for a Pontifical Biblical Institute, and with the Encyclical *Providentissimus,* which clearly asserts that the Bible has nothing to say in the field of natural science). It is to him that historical research owes the bold flinging open of the Vatican archives to scholars of all nations and creeds, with the expressed wish that historians should say nothing untrue and hide nothing of the truth, even though it should be to the detriment of the Church and the Papacy. After the negative interventions of earlier Popes against the Bible Societies, and the prohibition of Bible reading by the laity except by permission of the Inquisition (which had been renewed by Gregory XVI in 1836) came Leo XIII's positive call for private Bible reading in the vernacular.

There were even, under Leo XIII, some faint beginnings of a positive renewal of the liturgy: a constructive approach to the Missal and the Breviary with the astonishing creation of new prefaces, etc.; and, in connection with Leo's revision of the Index in 1897, the lifting of the ban, renewed by Pius IX, on the translation of the Canon of the Mass into the vernacular.

Similarly, there was an awakening of the Ecumenical Movement. More than one of Leo's encyclicals was devoted to the reunion of separated Christians. After Pius IX's clumsily-expressed invitation to those separated from Rome to come to the Vatican Council, and the ugly words used of Protestants at the Council itself, it is striking to find Leo XIII's reunion encyclical *Praeclara* avoiding the traditional terminology of "schism", "heresy" and "sect" and addressing Protestants as "beloved brothers". Leo was particularly concerned with the Eastern Church, and in this connection praised the missionary methods of SS. Cyril and Methodius, which had been under fire in the earlier period.

Some of these reforming measures were large, some small. But in any case they constituted a considerable beginning of renewal. The fact that the Catholic Church is no longer something dumped in the midst of the modern world like a lump fallen out of the Middle Ages; the fact that she has gone over from a onesided, reactionary defence to a hopeful offensive and renewal, that she has developed unsuspected energies, that Catholics have overcome their inferiority complex in an energetic work of revival, is all to a great extent the achievement of Leo XIII.

Renewal in the Church has made significant advances along many paths since Leo XIII. What a difference there is between the Catholic Church under Leo X (Luther's Pope) and Leo XIII; but what a difference, again, between the

Church in 1878, when Leo XIII became Pope, and in 1958, when John XXIII became Pope! We think we have the right to say, and we shall return to it again, that while she has held fast to all that is essentially Catholic, and while it is true that many deficiencies remain, yet the Catholic Church of 1961 is in whole areas of her life a reformed and renewed Catholic Church.

And we might here, very quietly, ask ourselves the question, if Martin Luther had lived in the Catholic Church of today, what course would he have followed? Is it absolutely certain that that course would have taken him out of the Church?

But this is by the way (and meant only as a hint that the protests appropriate then cannot remain, without further examination, today's protests). What is important is not what Luther would have done, but what we are doing. What is important is not whether Luther would sever himself from us today, but whether *we* can come together again. And so we come to the all-important question:

4. HOW CAN CATHOLICS AND PROTESTANTS COME TOGETHER AGAIN?

(1) The right way is the way on which John XXIII has set out: through renewal of the Church to reunion. We have already spoken of

what this means: for the renewal of the Church, and through this for reunion, we can suffer, pray, criticize, act. But what does "act" mean at this present moment?

(a) Not passive appeals to return to the unity of the Church.

We do not think of ourselves as well content and wholly self-sufficient while our brethren around us have to seek for what they need and do not have. We are thankful to be able to say, openly, that we owe many insights to Protestant theology which we should be sorry to have to do without. It is true that an Instruction of the Holy Office (20 Dec. 1949) says of converts, "Things must not be presented in such a way as to give the impression that by their entry into the Church they bring her something essential which she has hitherto lacked." These words, which have often given offence, must be rightly understood. Converts do not bring with them anything of the fundamental, essential substance of truth which the Church did not have before; but they can enrich her greatly with a more fully developed and realized vision of truth, as the example of great converts shows . . . Hence we cannot help feeling painfully distressed when representatives of the Church's teaching authority, or Catholics in general, assume a rigidly narrow attitude of pseudo-infallibility. They are not then representing the true nature of the Church, but only the inadequacy of the "earthen vessels" in her.[1]

Four hundred years of fruitless appeals to the Protestants, and nine hundred of fruitless appeals to the Orthodox, are perhaps demonstration enough that this is no way to reach the goal. It cannot be a matter simply of the others' "returning", as though we had no responsibility for the split, as though *we* therefore had nothing to make good, as though it were not in the least up to *us* to go to meet them, and as though they had nothing whatever to bring with them—they, our brothers, lovers of Christ our Lord! There is altogether too much self-glorification and self-righteousness in such behaviour, however much it may be accompanied by prayer. We are not merely to say "Lord, Lord", but to do the will of the Father. What is demanded of us is not a faith which waits inertly for the others to return but faith active through love (Gal. 5.6), faith which goes to meet them. This is what the Pope wants.

(b) Not simply individual conversions. It is part of the Catholic faith that God wills that *all* men shall be saved; no one is lost unless by his own fault. As Pius IX clearly pointed out,[2]

[1] Cardinal Döpfner, "Kirche Christi unterwegs", *Una Sancta*, 12 (1957), 6.

[2] See Denzinger, *Enchiridion Symbolorum*, no. 1647.

this statement is to be understood in the sense
that those who are "in invincible ignorance",
i.e., in good faith, outside the organized Catholic
Church, can attain eternal salvation. Of course,
it is constantly happening (and often in very
strange ways) that a non-Catholic comes to see a
greater fullness of light shining in the Catholic
Church; that he comes to recognize, despite all
her numerous deficiencies, that she preserves
the wholeness of Christianity, with the apostolic
and Petrine succession, in a way that other communions, lacking the apostolic or Petrine succession, despite all the good that is in them,
do not. Such a man will not fail to follow the
voice of his conscience. It is clear that conversion
can be the solution to any number of conflicts
in the individual conscience; and that this can,
in particular, be true of a difficult situation
which is, alas, misunderstood in purely Catholic
countries, namely that of a mixed marriage. But
these individual conversions, important as they
are, and valuably as they have enriched the
Church (think for instance of Newman, Jörgen-
sen, Van de Pol, Bouyer, Schlier, all the author-
converts, etc.), offer no kind of solution to schism
itself. Our four hundred, our nine hundred
years, have surely demonstrated that individual
conversions do not reunite our communions. All
too often, on the Catholic side, we have simply
counted conversions to the Catholic Church and

given no thought to what was happening in the
opposite direction; nor let ourselves consider, as
we counted, the cases of all those who, finding
themselves involved in conflict, have simply
given up all their religious affiliations; nor,
above all, remembered to count the ever-mounting figure of the unconverted. The little number
of conversions simply does not weigh in the
balance, in practice, against that ever-mounting
figure. The Pope does not simply want individuals to come over; he wants the reunion of
our separated Christian communions.

(c) Not simply "moral reform". In answer to
the question "What can we Catholics do about
reunion?" one now and then hears the answer
"Be a better Catholic!", and a reference to Matt.
5.16: "So let your light shine before men that
they may see your good works and glorify your
Father who is in heaven." It is a very good
answer, but must not be misunderstood. What
is "being a better Catholic", as sometimes understood? Keeping the Commandments better, not
lying, not swearing, not stealing, not calumniat-
ing, not committing adultery, taking more part
in the Church's life, etc.? Obviously, we have to
do this all the time. But we have to do it *all* the
time, it is our *unending* task, precisely because
it is concerned with man's *unending* imperfection and sinfulness in this world. Our schism, on
the other hand, goes back not simply to the

weakness and evil concupiscence in human
nature but (making full allowance for the guilt
involved) to a particular historical event independent of any individual living today. It is not,
like the seven deadly sins, a part of the *unending*
sinfulness of man in this world; it came about
historically and, unlike the seven deadly sins, it
can, by the grace of God, be brought to an end.
But this calls not merely for general moral improvement but for special efforts directed to this
particular end. So, "be a better Catholic", by
all means, but in what way? A better Catholic
in regard to our separated brethren! More precisely, in regard to the justified demands of our
separated brethren. And this brings us to our
positive point.

(d) Not these things, but the renewal of the
Catholic Church, drawing on the resources of
her own essential nature, through the meeting
of all that is justified in Protestant demands and
criticisms.

> While it is true to say "The light of our
> holy Mother the Church shines undimmed by
> any fault", it is equally true to say, with
> Bishop Keppler, "The urge to reform is in-
> born in the Church from the beginning."
> Hence it is the duty of her pastors to be wide
> awake and wide open to the efforts of the
> Ecumenical Movement as it strives to find its
> way; it is their task to see that the holiness of

Christ's Church shall become powerfully visible to all those who call upon the name of the Lord. We want our Christian brethren to be able to sense that their longing for Christ's justifying grace, entirely the work of the Holy Spirit, whose presence in them we discern and reverence, finds its full scope, and indeed its fulfilment, within the Catholic Church.[1]

To whatever extent the Protestant protest is justified, it is the Catholic Church herself, against whom the protest is made, who must take it up and provide the remedy which will make the protest pointless. True, the Church, being of men and of sinners, will remain an *ecclesia reformanda* until the end of time. But surely she, who, to name but one example, accepted what was valid in both Nestorianism and Monophysitism at the Council of Chalcedon, must not fail to do justice too, now that the age of polemic is blessedly over, to the demands of the Reformers; so that the Catholic Church may be truly an *ecclesia reformata*, a reformed Church, not absolutely and in every respect, but so far as the challenge of the Reformation is concerned. *Ecclesia catholica reformata*: what course of action would then be followed by those who have separated themselves from us, the ancient Church, precisely for the sake of Church reform?

[1] Cardinal Döpfner, "Kirche Christi", 7.

(2) It is hoped that all this will be rightly understood; i.e., not onesidedly but with a proper balance. If a Protestant were jubilantly to conclude that all this means a belated imitation of the Reformation on the part of the Catholic Church, he would be overlooking a number of points:

(a) That the Catholic Church has, as we Catholics believe, remained essentially true to herself; that she has pursued her own course of renewal and reform, in continuity with her past and without any revolutionary convulsion, and so preserved the irreducible substance of Catholicism; that she has done this not by her own power but by the power of the Spirit of Jesus Christ, who preserves her in the truth.

(b) That Protestantism too has undergone a not inconsiderable development, and is today in the midst of a reformation of the Reformation—as indeed it cannot fail to be. For it seems (at least to a Catholic) that there is no more dangerous description that a Church could claim for itself than "reformed". To call oneself a "Reformed Church" (whether Calvinist or Lutheran) could well represent a rejection of all further reformation; we *are* reformed, and now it's up to the others, Catholics in this case, to be reformed too! Is it as simple as that? Is a protesting summons to "reform", unaccompanied by deeds, by any admission of guilt or error (including those of the Reformers), or by any proposals for remedy and improvement, any more Christian than a Catholic summons to return to the unity of the Church equally unaccompanied by deeds? Might not this too be self-glorifying and self-righteous Pharisaism (the Pharisees thought of themselves as "reformed Israel"!), even though it were accompanied by prayer? Could individual conversions or "moral reform" be regarded as a solution to the problem from this side, either? What happens when a protest is raised to a principle—can it not be as paralysingly soporific as anything else?

"Surely Protestantism, Lutheranism, is really a corrective; and the result of having made Protestantism into the regulative has caused great confusion", as Kierkegaard says.[1] Has not the corrective become, to a large extent, even the constitutive element of the whole? A Catholic would hardly dare to go so far as this quotation from Hermann Kutter, the Zürich theologian, pastor of Neumünster, with which Walter Nigg ends his essay on Luther:[2]

The task of Luther's true heirs is to take fresh thought for the prophetical duty of criticism, as Hermann Kutter has pointed out:

[1] *The Journals of Søren Kierkegaard*, ed. and trans. A. Dru, Oxford, 1938, p. 509.

[2] Walter Nigg, *Das Buch der Ketzer*, Zürich, 1949, p. 350.

"I believe that if Luther and Zwingli were to rise from their graves today, they would drive us from our building-sites and say: We know you not, for all your fine Centenary Essays and Reformation celebrations. You are not Protestants, you make no protest of your own, you only keep on celebrating ours . . . Have you nothing better to do than protest against the Catholic Church, and make idols of the words we used, as old tools and weapons are enshrined in museums? They are good for looking at, but not for use; it is new ones that are needed. Where then are your new weapons, where the embattled array of your modern foes? Do you not see that what we said in our day must be said today—not in the same words, but the same spirit—to our mammon-worshipping society: the Justice of God? . . . Do penance, cast off your shilly-shallying, lift yourselves out of your shadow-life, make your protest not against the spectres of the past, which have nothing to do with your day, but against that Enemy who rules this age . . ."

"The Reformation is still going on!" said Schleiermacher. Well and good, but it does not necessarily have to proceed in Schleiermacher's direction. Perhaps a Catholic theologian who honestly tries to be frank on the subject of his

own Church, and who does his best to understand the problems and desires of Protestants,
may be forgiven for frankly and fraternally
speaking his mind. Catholics often ask: "Is the
Ecumenical Movement any use, is the Council
going to be any use, do Protestants *want* to
understand us, do they really want to come to
meet us?" I have always answered, Yes, and with
complete conviction. There is indeed no end to
the good will to be found amongst Protestants.
Of course there are also plenty of variations to
be found amongst them, including some back-
slidings into out-of-date polemics over what has
already become common ground. But over and
above this, there are certain questions which
cause us an ever-recurrent, painful embarrass-
ment, as: Is it not still the case that "Catholicizing" is the deadliest of all sins to a true
Protestant? Is it not true that every sort of
"liberalizing" is allowed, so long as it does not
lead in the direction of the Catholic Church?
Is one not free to deny or minimize the divinity
of Christ, and "interpret" his resurrection away
to nothing, so long as one does not show too
much understanding of the New Testament witness to a Petrine or episcopal office? Is it not the
case that risk of dismissal or other proceedings
for unorthodoxy exists in one direction only? Is
there not a tendency to look favourably towards
Moscow, simply to avoid having to look favourably towards Rome? What is one to say about

all this, and much else besides? Catholics of the
nineteenth century, particularly in Germany,
suffered from a multiple inferiority-complex in
face of the achievements of Protestantism at that
date; it was often this that held them back from
uninhibited, positive, creative action. Has the
wheel come full circle? Are Protestants trying
to immunize themselves against the impressive-
ness of the present-day Catholic Church to the
point of having a fixation about compromise?

We should like to beg our Protestant brothers,
all our Protestant brothers everywhere, that they
will, on their side too, keep themselves open
towards the Catholic Church and the demands
she makes, and come to meet us in brotherly
love. We shall have to count on this kind of
openness and this kind of coming half-way, if
what we ourselves do for the sake of reunion is
to have any meaning.

How can Catholics and Protestants come together? We said before, through a renewal of
the Church. But this does not only mean a
Catholic reform doing justice to all that is valid
in Protestant demands. It also means a Protestant reform doing justice to all that is valid in
Catholic demands. It does *not* mean playing
down the truth, soft-pedalling our differences,
making false syntheses and easy compromises,
but self-searching, self-criticism, self-reform—in
the light of the Gospel of Jesus Christ, and with

our separated brothers in mind. If Catholics carry out Catholic reform and Protestants carry out Protestant reform, both according to that Gospel image, then, because the gospel of Christ is but one, reunion need not remain a utopian dream. Reunion will then be neither a Protestant "return" nor a Catholic "capitulation", but a brotherly approach from both sides, with neither consciously calculating, on the other's behalf, which of them has more steps to take; an approach penetrated through and through with love, and wholly determined by truth.

Will there be on both sides—among Church leaders, theologians and lay-people—enough men of goodwill, ready to go, step by step, along a road which is going to be neither particularly short nor particularly easy? We can take courage and hope from the fact that some important steps have been taken already, even by the Catholic Church, for long believed to be without any positive interest in the challenge of the Ecumenical Movement.

5. CATHOLIC STEPS TOWARDS POSITIVE FULFILMENT OF THE VALID DEMANDS OF THE REFORMERS

Life can never be fully expressed in words; the mysterious life of the Church least of all. We cannot possibly state all that has been going on invisibly in the privacy of men's hearts, all that has been quietly accomplished in unspectacular work by individuals, to make genuine Catholic renewal a reality; every element in it modifies the whole life of the Church, and therefore has its share in the credit for the fact that the Catholic Church of today, unlike that of the Reformation period, is to a great extent a renewed, reformed Church. But there are particular little lights, prominent here and there, which certainly are not the whole of the Church's life, but do at least sketch the outline of the renewed Catholic Church of today. It is not suggested that these lights bathe the Church in a rosy glow; the preceding chapters should have dealt with any such suspicion. But they can serve to indicate how far a general reform of the Church has gone forward, not only between Leo X and Leo XIII but between Leo XIII and John XXIII. Very quietly, without saying much about it, the Church of the last sixty years has been taking definite steps in self-renewal, and thus at the same time advancing to meet our Protestant brothers. There was practically no intention of making any such advance. It was rather a matter of a genuine Catholic renewal, not on the whole envisaging Protestants but aiming, in the sight of the Lord, at a fuller realization of the riches of Catholicism. But though no approach was intended, it was none the less made. It has been so large, that the two sides of the schism, each in their separate senses "re-formed", have, with all their differences, become not unlike each other.

Many of the steps forming this process are in themselves small; but taken all together they add up to a fair distance. We have to give due importance here to small things; we shall be listing (sometimes in telegraphically summary style) a number of apparently dull and irrelevant details, but they amount to a great deal when taken all together. Compared with the Reforma-tion, one might, taking them individually, laugh at them as "pocket-size reforms". But no attentive observer of the life of the Catholic Church in these last decades could fail to see that these individual measures of renewal, typically Catholic, i.e., slow, as they have been, do, taken together, amount to a real, full-scale Reform. It is after all possible that the man who plods the long way round, taking the seemingly easy and well-marked line of ascent, will get to the top just as surely as the man who rushes at short cuts—and without the risk of breathless-ness and exhaustion, let alone getting lost or falling.

One can hardly pay too much attention (this applies especially to theologians) to the require-ments of reform at the practical, concrete level. It was these, and not simply abstract theological propositions, which fired the Reformation, and they are equally the determining factor if we are to come together again. Theology, of course, has a central significance. But a Protestant theologian must beware of reducing the demands of the Reformation to some one basic principle (such as the primacy of the Word, or of grace, or the sovereignty of God, etc.) and then taking a rigid stand upon it. This would be to overlook (a) that it is highly dubious procedure to reduce all the disputed points to some one theological principle and then to build up a theological system (which would then be polemical in aim) on *that* rather than on Revelation as a whole; (b) that it is easy to set up abstract theological principles (and, quite often, to get your opponent to agree to them), but that what matters is both how they are then interpreted theologically and how they are applied in the life of the Church; (c) that it is not enough to establish what were the theological insights of the Reformation period without also enquiring into their sometimes highly dubious development in the course of Protestant history.

Hence we should prefer, precisely from the theological point of view, to base ourselves not only on the theoretical but also on the practical manifestations of the Catholic Church's life; from which, ultimately, formal theological principles will emerge (perhaps, indeed, the primacy of the Word and of grace, and the sovereignty of God). As we briefly enumerate these Catholic steps towards a fulfilment of Protestant ideals, we hope that they will be read as a concrete invitation, on the part of Catholics, to our Protestant brothers not to stand pat on their own "Reformed Church" but to go on reforming the Reformation in such a way as to come, lovingly and fraternally, to meet us.

What, then, are these reforming ideals which the Church has been working to achieve, if not completely, yet effectually, during the last seventy years—approximately, since Leo XIII, but presupposing the reforms of the earlier period? We shall begin with one that underlies much of the rest:

(1) Catholic appreciation of the *religious* motives in the Protestant Reformation.

It is true that, with few exceptions, present-day Catholic efforts to reform do not go back directly to any Protestant impulse. Nevertheless, a positive understanding of the genuinely religious demands in the Protestant Reformation has been extremely important for Catholic reform; because nothing else could bring down the seemingly necessary defensive wall of polemics and enable Catholics to learn something from the experiences, positive and negative, of Protestant reform.

Catholic understanding of the Reformation has developed to a significant degree. Consider

6 + c.a.r.

the progress in the judgements passed on Luther
himself, from Eck, Cochlaeus, and Bellarmine,
via Möhler, Döllinger, Jansen, Denifle, Grisar
and Reiter, down to Lortz and Jedin! For Döllinger, in his earlier writings, Luther was a
criminal; for Denifle, a man in whom nothing
godly can be found; for Grisar, a psychopath;
but for Lortz, a tragic individual, caught in
almost insoluble interior and exterior difficulties, and living by faith. Of course prejudices
and more or less popular polemical writings
still abound; but Lortz's epoch-making work on
the Reformation in Germany has nevertheless
established itself plainly in face of them all. And
this implies appreciation of the Reformation
as a religious phenomenon; admission that it
was, in a certain relative sense, necessary; admission of a share by Catholics in the guilt;
understanding of Luther as a religious personality; reduction of anti-Protestant feeling.

There has not only been historical research
to bring increased understanding of the Reformation. There has been a living approach of the
different communions to each other through
their common experience of persecution and
war, and their common fight against totalitarianism in its various forms and general dechristianization. Finally, there have been discussions in
common between Church leaders, theologians,
exegetes and laymen; ecumenical "workshops"

in many German cities, meetings of Catholic and Protestant publicists, co-operation within various institutions and organizations, joint theological study groups and exegetical congresses.

There will, on the other hand, have to be a certain amount of patient making allowances in the case of purely Catholic and consequently isolated countries like Spain and some of the South American states. We all know that the anti-Protestant measures taken in some of these countries are in no way approved by other Catholics. Yet much of it becomes understandable (not excusable) by reference to some of the factors involved: the traditional entanglement of the religious question with that of national unity (in Spain particularly); the infinitesimally small number of native-born Protestant Christians in these countries (most Catholics there know Protestantism only by inadequate hearsay); the often more than questionable missionary methods of some of the American sects (who bring the real Protestant communions into disrepute); finally the (not altogether intelligible) concentration of Protestant missionary efforts on these Catholic countries (what would the Swedes say if Rome organized massive missionary and financial resources for the conversion of Sweden while there were still plenty of unbaptized persons elsewhere?) Even in these

countries, Spain in particular, there is a growing
understanding of the Ecumenical Movement,
which has been given splendid encouragement
by the announcement of the Ecumenical Council. But we cannot expect prejudices to be
abolished in a single day, in Spain any more
than in Sweden.

For the rest, since to do full justice to all the
facts and points of view involved would need a
separate book, we must be content with summary indications in telegram-style:

(2) Growing regard for the Scriptures in the
Catholic Church. In the field of scholarship,
unlooked-for development in Catholic exegesis;
vast increase in biblical publications; lexicons,
commentaries, scriptural periodicals, populariza-
tions; steadily growing influence of scriptural
exegesis on Catholic dogma and preaching, leading to significant rearrangements in the hierarchy
of ideas; pioneer work in the two Pontifical
Biblical Institutes, at Rome and Jerusalem; encouragement of scientific exegesis in the encyclicals of Leo XIII and, especially, Pius XII, whose
Divino Afflante Spiritu (1943) shows how far the
Catholic Church of today goes in accepting
modern exegetical methods; along with this,
tacit correction or reinterpretation of anti-
modernist decrees on the Pentateuch, the
Johannine Comma, the Synoptic Problem, etc.
(cf. the detailed answer of the Secretary of the

Biblical Commission to Cardinal Suhard, 16 Jan. 1948); clear recognition of the authority of the original text, which, according to *Divino Afflante Spiritu*, "has greater authority and weight than any translation, however excellent, be it ancient or modern"; hence a definite decrease in the importance of the Vulgate, whose authenticity, as defined at Trent, may, according to the same encyclical, be regarded as juridical, not critical, and whose practical importance has been greatly lessened by Pius XII's introduction of the new Latin translation of the Psalms (especially in the Breviary); exegetical work in co-operation with Protestants, in which (as combined exegetical congresses have shown) differences in the doctrinal basis of interpretation have been almost indiscernible (which is perhaps a better indication of the relation of Scripture to tradition in both communions than any number of theoretical distinctions); finally, balanced, non-polemical interpretations of the relationship between Scripture and Tradition, as laid down at Trent.

In the life of the Catholic population, papal encouragement for translations from the original text, which are now plentiful in all civilized languages; numerous exhortations by the Pope and bishops to private reading of the Holy Scriptures (Pius X's recommendations of daily Bible reading); dissemination of the Bible amongst the people, which has greatly increased, not least through the activities of the Catholic Bible Associations, whose work has spread as far afield as Spain and South America; widespread interest among Catholics in biblical lectures, study-groups and preaching; recognition by Pius XII of the efforts of the Bible Associations, in contrast to Pius IX's rejection of Bible Societies.

(3) Development of Catholic liturgy into a people's liturgy. The theoretical basis: significant increase in theological attention to the Eucharist as a memorial celebration; as a banquet; as the community worship of the people, who have, in their own fashion, a priesthood; more balanced interpretation of the meaning of transubstantiation and sacrifice; more profound and less juridical statement of the Church's teaching.

The practical application: Pius X's epoch-making pronouncements on the people's participation in the liturgy, on frequent Communion, and child Communion; enormous increase in the use of the Missal, according to his principle of "not praying *at* Mass, but praying the Mass"; effectual, explicit recovery of the communal character of the Mass by the Dialogue Mass and various adaptations; especially in Germany, making use of prayers and singing in common; extensive use of the vernacular in the administration of the sacraments and the burial of the

dead; use of the vernacular for almost the whole
of the parish Mass (though in this case always
simultaneously accompanied by celebration in
Latin by the priest); in 1949, papal permission
for the priest himself to use Chinese for the
whole of the Mass except the Canon (the same
permission has been given for Hebrew); further
important reforms by Pius XII—permission for
evening Mass, both on Sundays and weekdays,
far-reaching relaxation of the fasting laws, and
the renewal, full of promise of more to come, of
the liturgy of Holy Week, especially the Easter
Vigil; discouragement (partly on account of
evening Mass) of subjective "devotions", sometimes of doubtful value, in favour of the common
liturgy of the Church; pioneer "path-finding"
work on liturgical reform done by national and
international liturgical congresses; the reform
of the Breviary (and the Mass) which Rome has
undertaken, for which the simplification of the
rubrics, already in operation, is a preparation;
appreciation of the value of congregational singing, with cultivation of the great tradition of
German Church music, adoption of a considerable number of Protestant hymns, fresh musical
adaptation of liturgical psalm-singing in French
with the Gelineau settings (which have been
taken up in Spain, and introduced into
England), and parallel German experiments;
extreme simplification of modern Catholic

churches, with altars of table form; corresponding simplification of vestments and liturgical objects, and a shedding of superfluous pomp.

(4) Understanding of the universal priesthood: (a) in theory: the priesthood of all the faithful is one of the favourite themes in current Catholic theology (a large number of significant publications have appeared on the theology of the laity); Pius XII, in his encyclicals on the Church (*Mystici Corporis*) and the liturgy (*Mediator Dei*) gave impressive teaching on the lofty meaning of the universal priesthood alongside the hierarchical priesthood; the dignity of marriage, of the vocation of the citizen, of the whole life of the Christian in the world and of earthly realities are all receiving theological attention (note in this connection the working out of the distinction between Catholic Action and the action of Catholics).

(b) In practice: Catholic Action, despite its subordination to the Hierarchy and its occasional clericalist deviations, represents a huge strengthening of the lay element in the Church; and this is something entirely new in the Church since Trent. Theology, especially at German universities, is being more and more studied by lay people, who are becoming increasingly important in catechetical work. The foundation of secular institutes has suggested an appropriate contemporary form for total participation of lay people in the life of the Church today. The various lay congresses, especially the two World Congresses of the Lay Apostolate at Rome, have shown that the Church's leaders are becoming more and more aware of the significance of the laity in the Church. Discussions about the layman's status in canon law, about lay deacons and the revival of the conferring of minor orders, even about laymen in the College of Cardinals, show that the position of the laity in the Church has by no means reached the term of its development.

(5) Numerous other points which deserve more detailed treatment than they can have here:

(a) Increased adaptation of the Church to the nations, and discouragement of Europeanism and Latinism in the missions; rejection of Europeanism in principle in the missionary encyclicals of Benedict XV (*Maximum Illud*, 1919) and Pius XI (*Rerum Ecclesia*, 1926); consecration of native bishops; erection of established hierarchies in China, India, Africa (with a cardinal for each); repeal of the decree resulting from the unhappy Chinese Rites Dispute by the authorization of the civil ancestor cult in Japan (by Pius XI in 1936) and of the civil Confucius cult in China (1939); a growing understanding and sympathy for the Eastern Church, and the various rites and liturgical languages (celebration of the Greek Liturgy in St. Peter's in the presence of the Pope).

6*

(b) Far-reaching purifications of the Papacy from politics by the Lateran Treaties and official renunciation of all claim to the Papal State; by the various concordats, in so far as they call for abstention on the part of the Church from matters which are purely the affair of the State; by concentration on the part of the Popes in this century on pastoral and religious questions.

(c) Beginning of a new reform of the Curia under Pius X: reorganization of the Roman Congregations and Courts (reduction of the Congregations from twenty to eleven, making for greater simplicity and ease of supervision; elimination of overlapping jurisdiction, thorough separation of administrative and judicial powers, improvement in administration and rectification of abuses); reform of procedure in ecclesiastical courts; economic reforms in the Vatican (levelling of salaries, abolition of various superfluous posts); considerable abolition of outmoded etiquette; reform of the law on papal elections (abolition of the Exclusive); reorganization of pastoral work in Rome (the post of Vicar General, the suburban diocese, pastoral visitation); continuation of this reform under Pius XII by increasing the international element in the College of Cardinals.

(d) Codification and simplification of the canon law of the Latin Church by Pius X and Benedict XV, and the corresponding codification, not yet complete, of the canon law of the Eastern Church.

(e) A growing understanding of the value of tolerance, not only among Catholics at large but at the summit, as was shown in Pius XII's famous address on this subject in 1953.

(f) A growing understanding in moral theology of the claims of the individual conscience (also expressed in the canonization of Joan of Arc) and of the ever-varying situation of the individual.

(g) Of particular importance for reunion: suspension of celibacy, in individual cases, by Pius XII, by permitting the ordination to the priesthood of certain married ex-Protestant pastors, and thus allowing married priests (with full freedom to use their marriage) even in the Western Church. Implied in this is the recognition, in practice, that it is possible for a divine vocation to the ministry to manifest itself, and develop, in one of our brothers who is separated from the Catholic Church.

(6) Concentration and interiorization of the devotional life of the ordinary Catholic. All the above factors in Catholic reform, especially the liturgical-biblical-pastoral-missionary renewal, have brought about an advance (still insufficient, but none the less visible) in that concentration of popular piety which was one of the desires of the Reformers. All that is secondary in Catholic

devotion (relics, indulgences, veneration of the
saints, and much else that was overstressed at
the time of the Reformation) has been mani-
festly giving ground, especially amongst those
who are most actively Catholic, in favour of
what is primary in our faith; in favour, first and
foremost, of a liturgical, biblical, Christocentric-
ally and theocentrically shaped and interiorized
piety. Despite all our defects, which we have not
tried to hide, it is impossible to ignore the great
upsurge in the religious life of the Catholic
Church in this century. This again is a matter
in which we must have patience, and not expect
the same from an uneducated Catholic as from
an educated one, or from a southern temperament as from a northern, or from countries
which have no vital contact with the challenge
of Protestantism the same as from those which,
having a mixture of confessions within them,
are in many respects more aware of these matters. In any case, positive developments in this
field are to be found everywhere; and the future
depends more on the formative Catholic elite
than on the often dragging feet of the Catholic
masses. In mixed countries like ours, we are constantly able to affirm the similarity that has
developed between the spirituality of leading
Catholics and of leading Protestants; and spirituality is more important than any number of
divisive externals. Over and over again, Catholics and Protestants who get to know each other

better realize with astonishment how alike—
despite their remaining differences—they have
become. It is a likeness founded ultimately upon
our faith in one Father through one Jesus Christ
in one Holy Spirit; in our praying of the same
Lord's Prayer and the same psalms, our meditation and study of the same Holy Scriptures, our
life nourished by the same baptism, the same
Spirit and the same—still too little realized—
great common Christian tradition.

This chapter was not an attempt to describe
the whole spiritual situation of the Catholic
Church today. But it should have made it clear
that she has in this century gone far along the
road towards a meeting-point, that she has reformed herself in the most various ways and
that she has thereby made a whole series of
beginnings on the positive fulfilment of the
valid demands of the Reformation.

But what about the most important and the
most difficult matter of all: the renewal, the
reform of theology, of doctrine?

6. THE QUESTION OF DOCTRINE

The expression "reform of doctrine" is not,
generally speaking, used amongst Catholics. It
is one that can, in point of fact, cause as much
confusion as clarification. All too often, those
undertaking a "reform of doctrine" have been

those who thought themselves called to give a
new form to the Christian revelation, according
to their own needs and prejudices and without
reference to any Church or tradition, so as to
formulate, in accord with the spirit of the times,
some sort of incorrupt "essence of Christianity".
"Reform of doctrine" in this case means, in
practice, a *selection* from the totality of Revelation; which is, precisely, heresy. Furthermore,
as it is commonly understood the word "reform"
presupposes some *de*formation. Deformation of
doctrine in *theology* (whether directly heretical
or inclining towards heresy) is not in the least
unthinkable for a Catholic; on the contrary,
history shows that, because of men's deficiencies,
it has happened only too often. But the situation
is different when we come to the Church's
dogma: for the Church is the chosen herald and
witness of Jesus Christ himself (Matt. 28.18–20;
Luke 10.16; John 17.17 f.; Acts 1.8), taught by
the Holy Spirit (John 14.26; 16.13), the pillar
and ground of the truth. (1 Tim. 3.15.) We cannot speak of any "deformation" in the Church's
dogma, such as is possible in theology, nor, in
consequence, in this sense, of a "reform" of
doctrine. What the Catholic Church does recognize in her dogma is the giving of new forms or
more developed forms to a doctrine which has
not in every respect achieved its complete form;
as the Vatican Council defined it, a growth and

advance.[1] The Encyclical *Humani Generis*, too, says that the Church is not always unchanging in her use of technical terms; dogmatic formulae can be further polished and perfected.[2] These pronouncements rest upon two interrelated facts: that in the field of dogma, there is development, and there is polemic.[3]

There is a *development* of dogma, in the sense of an unfolding of what is implicit so as to make it explicit, under the influence of the Holy Spirit. Although dogmatic definitions express the truth with infallible accuracy and are in this sense unalterable (as against Modernism), yet they are by no means rigid, fossilized formulae. They form part of human history, with its limitations. What they express is indeed an objective view, but it is at the same time one that is historically conditioned; hence, as human, finite statements, they can never exhaust the mystery and the fullness of the divine revelation of truth. One and the same truth of faith can always be expressed in a still more complete, more adequate, better formula. Thus a truth that is, as it were, wrapped up in the particular

[1] Denzinger, *Enchiridion Symbolorum*, no. 1800.

[2] *Acta Apostolicae Sedis*, 42 (1950), 566; translated as *False Trends in Modern Teaching*, London, C.T.S., para. 16.

[3] Cf. the further treatment of this theme in H. Küng, *Rechtfertigung. Die Lehre Karl Barths und eine katholische Besinnung*, 2nd ed., Einsiedeln, 1957, pp. 105–27.

historical outlook of one age can be set free from it and placed in a wider, more adequate (but still finite) historical perspective.

Then there is a *polemic* of dogma; a positive struggle, with the weapons of argument, against one's opponent, accompanying one's own advance in the truth. Most dogmatic definitions have been drawn up against heresies and are thus neither more nor less than defensive barriers, and aids to a better understanding of a truth already possessed. The Church concentrates on the points endangered by heresy, and concentration of this sort always involves a certain narrowing. Certain aspects of the truth, because they are under fire, will be fully formulated and thus brilliantly illuminated, perhaps to the detriment of others which may sink into obscurity; it is always possible for any one decree to leave other, and perhaps highly important, aspects of a revealed truth in darkness. As G. de Broglie says,[1] the infallibility of the Church in her teaching office must not be mistaken for some "imaginary charism of universal insight". Definitions and decrees are simply not intended to say everything that there is to say about the truth in question. They are not intended as

[1] In his preface to L. Bouyer's *The Spirit and Forms of Protestantism*, London, 1956, p. x. Cf. the Papal Secretary of State, Cardinal Tardini, speaking of infallibility: "Non conferisce l'omniscienza al Papa." (*Osservatore Romano*, 1 Nov. 1959.)

balanced, detached, learned treatises but as corrections of particular, definite errors. This has, of course, a special bearing on the decrees framed against the doctrine of the Reformers at the Council of Trent.

Thus all theological formulae, even in the case of dogma, have quite definite limitations. This does not mean that a theologian, when dealing with a traditional formula that has been upheld and elaborated in the Church for centuries, can treat it lightly or substitute something else for it at will. But it is the serious duty of theologians to see all theological formulae and dogmas *against the background and in the context of revelation in its entirety, in both Old and New Testaments*; and (not failing to learn from our fellow-Christians separated from the Church, who, having that same common origin, are not without the truth) to see them ever more freshly, more adequately, and more fully. Thus it is possible, indeed constantly happens, that even "irreformable" utterances of the teaching office can, without ever being falsified, come to be seen in a better and more balanced way; they can in this sense be, not negatively but very positively, corrected and improved, as for example the Council of Chalcedon improved on the irreformable definition of the Council of Ephesus. All this amounts in fact to nothing other than a *renewal of doctrine*. This is more than a mere recovery of what may have been neglected. Even apart from neglected truths, the Church is faced in every age with theological questions and theological challenges which she has never met before. Hence what is required is a renewal in the most positive sense of the word: a forming and shaping anew, in every age, of the doctrine received in the Gospel as a mustard-seed, so that it shall reach its true Catholic stature and fullness. What is wanted is a renewal of doctrine that goes back and back to the sources, and thus shows forth the ancient doctrine as forever young, as the Encyclical *Humani Generis* says:

> This twofold spring of doctrine divinely made known to us contains, in any case, treasures so varied and so rich that it must ever prove inexhaustible. That is why the study of these hallowed sources gives the sacred sciences a kind of perpetual youth; avoid the labour of probing deeper and deeper yet into the sacred deposit, and your speculations—experience shows it—grow barren.[1]

This gives us a description of what we should mean by a Catholic renewal of doctrine.

This, which has constantly happened and does happen, perfectly legitimately, in the Catholic

[1] Pius XII, *Humani Generis* (*False Trends in Modern Teaching*), para. 21.

Church, would doubtless be called by our Protestant brethren a "reform" of doctrine. They
do not in general mean by this, any more than
we do, some sort of relativist destruction and
dissolution of dogma (as for instance that of the
ancient councils), without reverence or reference
to Tradition. Although, as before, we prefer the
word "renewal" because of its more positive
emphasis, we do not need to raise any difficulty
over a matter of terminology, provided that
"reform" is taken as having the fully positive
meaning described above. We shall only have to
take care that the "reform" of definitions—
which can rightly be called "irreformable"—
does not lead to the sacrifice of clarity. In doctrine as elsewhere we have to distinguish between what is given, *irreformably*, by God
through Jesus Christ in the Holy Spirit, and
what comes, *reformably*, from men. And what
was said before applies equally to doctrine: the
reformable and the irreformable cannot be adequately represented as being on two separate
levels. *Every* dogma of the Church expresses at
the same time both the irreformable divine revelation and what is human and reformable. There
are, indeed, in the Church's dogma, certain
abiding constants which remain in every possible
formula, through every variation of thought or
image or manner of speech, which are given to
us by God's revelation itself (as for example the

godhead and manhood of Jesus Christ), but there are not, properly speaking, any irreformable *areas* in what is of human, ecclesiastical formulation.

It is clear that renewal of doctrine is something that needs more detailed discussion by theologians. But it is not an empty principle devoid of practical application. It is a matter of real "reforms" such as would have seemed inconceivable to many Protestants in the past. This is shown, amongst many other things, by that very article of faith which was once regarded as the theological root of the schism of the Reformation, but which could scarcely serve today to bring about any division *from the Church* whatsoever: the doctrine of the justification of the sinner by God's grace.

Quiet "reforms" of this sort, despite the mountains of prejudice, misunderstanding and genuine difficulty which still lie between us, have brought about on many points, of recent years, not indeed an out-and-out identity between the Catholic and Protestant positions, but a considerable approximation of one to the other. Taking for granted our fundamental unity, never quite lost, about the Trinity, Christology and creation, this drawing-together has affected, first and foremost, the doctrine of sin and grace, but also those of Scripture and Tradition, and of the sacraments. A theological demonstration of this would be out of place here.[1]

But we have not yet reached the goal. It is not easy for two theologies which have lived separate lives for four hundred years to be assimilated to each other once more (even apart from divisions within Protestant theology itself). It is not easy —it often calls for wearisome exegetical and historical research—to unearth the reality, which may be one and the same, from under the words, which are different; to translate one's own concepts into those of the other man, and the other's back into one's own; and finally to produce a statement of some revealed truth which is balanced, intelligible to both sides, primarily scriptural in its orientation and at the same time not neglectful of Tradition. Endless efforts are still needed in theological discussion. What is wanted is not compromise, not disguising of disagreements, not shallow tolerance or colouring-over of truth with "charity"; there is but *one* truth: "*I am* the truth", says Christ (John 14.6), and "*The truth* shall make you free." (John 8.32.) But what is indeed wanted is to listen to the other side, to be carefully attentive, to be modestly enquiring, and finally

[1] References for numerous examples of how close many of our advanced positions have drawn to each other are given (especially for the benefit of the layman interested in theology) by H. Schütte, *Um die Wiedervereinigung im Glauben*, 2nd ed., Essen, 1959.

to be understanding in interpretation and so to discover the truth through love: "Doing the truth in charity, we may in all things grow up in him who is the head, even Christ." (Eph. 4.15.)

The complaint is quite often heard today that, while people in general are longing more and more for reunion, it is the theologians who are responsible for delaying it. Now, it is beyond question that theologians have acted, all too often, as though it were their job, and within their power, to find some definitive, explanatory, abstract formula for every single item in revelation, when they should often have been humbly content to let it rest in the varieties of scriptural utterance. Nevertheless, the accusation is ultimately unjust. It overlooks the fact that what we seek is a reunion in faith, which means in truth, and not in some vague, unfocused feeling of sympathy taking to itself the name of love. The theologian, on the other hand, will of course be aware of the grave dangers which may deprive his theological work of its ecumenical fruit.

(a) There is the danger of one's *personal mental blocks*. This can threaten the theologian in various ways: he may be so wrapped up in pure scholarship that he is indifferent to the needs of the Church; he may, out of intellectual laziness or sectarian pride, be entirely lacking in any deep concern for reunion; he may have an unconscious emotional bias against the other side, whether for personal reasons (family upbringing, education, conversion, unhappy experiences of those of the other faith, etc.), or from motives of denominational party-spirit (with an inferiority or superiority complex), or on theological grounds. Other serious blocks are indicated by the conviction that one has, fundamentally, nothing to learn from the other side; and by a sense of pleasure in having given nothing away in discussion or in having been "victorious" in controversy. Theological work for reunion may be crippled by the fear, ultimately rooted in unconscious insecurity, of having one's own orthodoxy shaken by a reconsideration of it; or again, finally, by having insufficient intellectual energy to break out of one's own theological scheme or system, constructed perhaps decades ago and defended ever since, as one must do if one is to remain ever open to the ever greater truth of divine revelation.

(b) The danger of identifying dogma with the opinion of a particular school. In contrast with other theological discussions, nothing should be put forward *as against the other side,* in any ecumenical discussion aimed at reunion, which is only an opinion freely held in some school, and not a teaching of the Church binding on all. That which divides schools from one another must not be made a cause of division from the Church. In this important matter, the Council of Trent, especially in its earlier period, offers a magnificent example for our imitation (it minimized scholastic opinions and scholastic language in favour of revealed truth and scriptural language). What accentuates this danger is that a theologian does not make the identification deliberately, but unawares; he *thinks* (with the best of intentions, but usually because of insufficiently thorough and uninhibited exegetical and historical research) that this or that statement is a universally binding doctrine of the Church, when it is in fact only an historically conditioned private or scholastic *opinion* about the doctrine of the Church. Hence it will always be one of our principal tasks in ecumenical discussion to work out, with the aid of every resource in scientific theology, what really is *de fide*, an article of faith. And so that we may not be too easily inclined to extend the area of binding faith, we may ask ourselves as a test, quite calmly, whether we would be ready to die for this or that statement; one accepts martyrdom for articles of faith, not for theological opinions. It is only in faith that the Church must have unity, not in theology. One Lord, one faith, one baptism (Eph. 4.5), but not, One theology! The Pope, in his inaugural encyclical on reunion, made express mention of the possibility and value of different theological views within the Church:

"We can do nothing against the truth, but for the truth" (2 Cor. 13.8). But there are many points which the Church leaves to the discussion of theologians, in that there is no absolute certainty about them, and, as the eminent English writer John Henry Cardinal Newman remarked, such controversies do not disrupt the Church's unity; rather they contribute greatly to a deeper and better understanding of her dogmas. These very differences shed in effect a new light on the Church's teaching, and pave and fortify the way to the attainment of unity.[1] There is a saying attributed to various sources and sometimes expressed in different words, but it is none the less true and unassailable. It runs: "Unity in essentials, freedom in uncertainties, in all things charity."[2]

(c) The danger of making excessive demands for theological agreement. It follows from the last point that in working to come together again in theology we must not demand an exaggerated degree of agreement. Otherwise we should, in our ecumenical discussions, be requiring some

[1] *Difficulties of Anglicans*, vol. 1, lect. x, pp. 261 f.
[2] Pope John XXIII, *Ad Petri cathedram*, trans. as *Truth, Unity and Peace*, London, C.T.S., 1959, pp. 21–2.

totally impossible kind of agreement which
would make reunion itself impossible. In discussing my book on justification (which asserts
that there is a fundamental agreement between
the Catholic and the Barthian doctrines of justification) Karl Rahner has made some remarks
that are extremely important with reference to
ecumenical discussion:

> Generally speaking, when two men reach
> agreement, having come together from *differ-
> ent* sides, and when this agreement is not
> based on some third, formal, binding authority
> accepted by both sides prior to their dispute
> [Rahner means the teaching authority of the
> Church], then this agreement is always of a
> precarious and risky nature, and can always
> be brought into question. Indeed, it is quite
> impossible to affirm it with ultimate certainty
> in any absolute sense, because each *formula
> concordiae* affirming that this agreement was
> one of realities and not only of words would
> need a further *formula concordiae formulae
> concordiae,* and so *ad infinitum.* But to say
> because of this that the agreement is "merely
> verbal" is absurd. An agreement about truth
> always takes place between human beings in
> a sociological *milieu,* and when it is attained
> *there,* it is, none the less, attained. But it is
> attained *there* when it is attained in words

and propositions (i.e., *verbally*, if you like) as used by men who pay attention to what they hear and think about what they say. It is not required of these men that they should try to peer into the inmost centre of each other's minds, where God alone sees and alone knows what is "really" being thought. There is a danger that, particularly in controversial theology, a neurotic fear that we are perhaps not "really", not "in our furthest depths", at one, may destroy such unity as might well exist. Such a fear then gives birth to that strange determination (noticeable in controversial theology) to prove the existence of disagreement by dint of ever more subtle and precise formulations, in cases where our sixteenth-century forebears, with less subtle formulae, would either have established a disagreement that anyone could easily see and express, or else affirmed their agreement. It is already the case today that *numerous* points of controversial theology call for the very highest flights of theological rhetoric in order to show the initiate (not the normal human being) just exactly where the difference lies. In such cases (there are of course many others of which the opposite is true) it would be better and more Christian to say that we are in agreement, or could at any rate reach agreement. As Barth has very courageously and soberly done. In order to have the right to live in separate Churches, we should have to be certain (to put it in broad general terms) that we were unmistakably disunited about the truth, and not merely be slightly uncertain whether we were really entirely at one, or just exactly what the other person really means, or whether we are quite sure that we have rightly understood him. This principle follows (it seems to me) on the one hand from our Christian duty to be united in one Church, and on the other from the essential impossibility of reaching absolute certainty about our ultimate interior identity of conviction. Such absolute certainty would presuppose an absolute certainty of the rightness of our own inmost belief in the sight of God, which seems to me as impossible and un-Catholic a thing as absolute certainty about our own righteousness in his sight. Perhaps those formulae of union in ancient times which seem somewhat artificial and political in their construction were not by any means the worst. What seems like a purely verbal and artificial unity may often be the one and only thing possible to men in face of the inconceivable Mystery: to find a formula which leaves to each side its own irreducible contribution to the controversy and to its solution, while requiring both to see and to

express that which was well-recognized by the
other but overlooked or not clearly seen by
himself, so that the other shall see that he
holds it too. We should not, then, say at once
of every formula of agreement: Oh, yes, but
just go a little deeper into it and discrepancies
will soon appear; the general terms in which
it is stated are simply hiding them! As though
we could not have the very same suspicion
about all the unity within the Catholic
Church![1]

7. WHAT ABOUT POPULAR PIETY?

The accusation that it is the *theologians* who
are holding up reunion is unjust on another
count as well: often it is not theology but popular piety (on both sides) which stands in the way
of reunion. Difficulties in this field are sometimes exaggerated: e.g., how long is it going to
take for our painstaking theological explanations
and reconciliations to work themselves into the
people's minds? etc., etc. In fact, on both sides,
the ordinary people are to a large extent in an
apathetic muddle about the actual *theological*
differences! The justification of the sinner is no

[1] K. Rahner, S.J., "Zur Theologie der Gnade. Bemer-
kungen zu dem Buche von Hans Küng: Rechtfertigung.
Die Lehre Karl Barths und eine katholische Besinnung",
in *Tübinger Theologische Quartalschrift*, 138 (1958),
40–77, esp. 48–50.

longer a subject of debate on highways and by-ways; how many average Catholics or average Protestants could give any moderately accurate account of the difference between the Lutheran and Tridentine doctrines of justification? The dechristianization which has thrust deep into all communions makes denominational differences seem irrelevant to many people today, in comparison with the fundamental difference between Christian and non-Christian. It is not necessary for reunion that the ordinary members of our congregations, who no longer know what the traditional controversies were about, should have the traditional theological difficulties explained to them at length in sermons and popular publications, so that they can then be told about the solutions which theologians have, with much labour, managed to achieve. In general, it is quite enough to give the people the positive truth, in all its Christian breadth and balance, and hence with an *implicit* fulfilment of the requirements of both sides in the controversy. What is required is not the stimulation of problems by special "ecumenical" preaching but the simple preaching of the Gospel, whole and unimpaired.

What has remained in the consciousness of the great mass of people is not so much theological controversy as the more external differences in popular piety. The problem of popular piety is far more difficult than it may seem at first sight, and we cannot do justice to it here. The theologian and the educated layman must beware of judging too "academically" here, and of ignoring or minimizing the variations in mass psychology and learning ability which the Church has to take into account if she hopes to be a people's Church and not that of an academic elite. The Church cannot simply abstract from the psyches of different populations and races, of the Latin and Germanic peoples, of men and women. Much that is right for one will be inadmissible for another. Much that would, in the mouth of a theologian who knew what he was saying, be heresy, is in the mouth of the people, whose faith is often better than its knowledge, truth—muddled, but still truth. This indulgence on the part of the Church is, it is true, a pedagogical attitude, but it is not ultimately based on any mere pedagogical theory; it is taken from the Scriptures. Jesus himself was indulgent towards relatively impure notions of faith, e.g., the woman with an issue of blood. (Luke 8.43-8.) It is not necessary to be a theologian in order to have true faith in the sight of God.

Obviously this does not mean that everything is to be tolerated. The permanent necessity for renewal and reform applies even more perhaps to popular piety than to anything else. For reunion it is quite unavoidable. Precisely because

in their judgement of other communions men
start from externals, it is vitally necessary that
these externals shall correspond as closely as
possible to the essence within. It is our never-
ending task to manifest anew the essence of our
faith. Hence it is the duty of the Church's
authorities to watch over popular piety, to set
up barriers against exaggerations and extrava-
gance, to correct false emphasis and distortion,
to root out superstitions and abuses. Here, as
always, reform must be not primarily negative
but positively creative: renewal, revival, interiorization, concentration of popular piety.

As we have stressed already, the Catholic
Church has made splendid progress in the renewal of popular piety, as part of her liturgical,
scriptural and pastoral renewal. That there is
still much to be done is obvious. And though
an ideal state of affairs is even more unattainable in popular piety than in most things, it
cannot be that "Catholic" superstition, often
medieval in form, linked to things justified in
themselves (pictures, statues, devotional objects,
novenas, indulgences, apparitions, pilgrimages,
etc.) must forever remain a byword amongst
Protestants. Though, while we are about it, those
who underline the superstition of others need
to see equally clearly the sheer unbelief amongst
themselves; superstition may still contain within it a hidden germ of faith, which unbelief

(often in surrender to more modern forms of superstition) has entirely lost. Nor can we allow ourselves to set up our own denomination as the better by a process of *oblique* comparison; it makes no sense to compare genuine piety within the Catholic Church with the neo-paganism of some Protestant countries, or with the eccentricities of certain Protestant sects; but nor is it sense to compare an imaginary ideal Protestantism with the reality of folk-Catholicism. We must never forget that there are on both sides— and mostly in corresponding degree—deficiencies and abuses in piety.

It would be still more dangerous if in our longing for renewal and reform we were to turn some particular type or form of piety into an absolute. *In dubiis libertas*, freedom in inessentials, applies to religious practice as well as to theology. A degree of emotion which would represent the utmost permissible limit for a Christian in Scandinavia might well be too little for a Christian in Italy. On the other hand, what may be genuine piety in Portugal or the South of France (in the matter of pictures, statues, prayers, processions, etc.) cannot be simply transferred to Germany. The Church has from the beginning loved unity in diversity. Reunion will be possible only if we strive to avoid imposing any uniformity on the practical piety of either communion. Yet it is perhaps in practical

7 + C.A.R.

piety that both have most to learn from each other. One welcome sign of this is the large number of Protestant hymns that have been taken into the Catholic hymn-book, while on the other hand many of the prayers in the Protestant service have their origin in the Roman Missal.

On the Protestant side, the chief difficulty in the way of our sharing a common life of prayer (it would be convenient but dishonest to ignore this) is Marian devotion. It was not always so. At the time of the Reformation, the attack was directed not so much against devotion to Mary as against the exuberances of the cult of the saints in general. Since then, many of the abuses and exaggerations in the veneration of the saints have been eliminated, and the Council of Trent defined it as useful and salutary but not as necessary and obligatory. Walter Nigg's book on "Great Saints", a book by a Protestant, much read by Catholics, has shown by its success amongst Protestant readers how much the situation over this matter has altered.

Protestant difficulties over Marian devotion, on the other hand, have accumulated more and more, not only because of the two Marian dogmas but also, and quite as much, over what we may call the Marian movement. Our Catholic theologians are called upon over and over again to defend the Church against charges of

"Marian maximalism" and "Marianism". We
are, so our critics tell us, neglecting Christ in
favour of Mary in all this flood of Marian books,
Marian sermons, Marian sodalities, Marian congresses, Marian apparitions, Marian pilgrimages;
we are exaggerating, both in theory and in practice, losing sight entirely of scriptural norms,
and isolating Mary from Christ on the one hand
and from Christians on the other. The accusations become still more grave when they seek to
explain these developments in terms of compara-
tive religion, religious psychology and religious
sociology.

Are all these accusations against our veneration of Mary without foundation? Heinrich
Fries has given a very carefully considered reply
in his *Answer to Asmussen*.[1] He indicates the
positive values in the Marian movement, but
admits "that we do see Marian maximalism
amongst us, and that it is by no means regarded
either as an unimportant or as a desirable thing,
but is causing real anxiety—not only to theologians in this country who say so publicly, but
to considerable sections of the Church, including
some at least of her pastors and leaders, if not
all of them."[2] He cites Peter Canisius, Doctor

[1] H. Fries, *Antwort an Asmussen*, Stuttgart, 1958
ch. 7: "Der marianische Maximalismus", pp. 127–54.
[2] Fries, *Antwort*, p. 142.

of the Church, who, while zealously defending veneration of Mary, also said:

> We recognize that things have crept into the cult of Mary which disfigure it, and that they may do so again. It is our special wish that the pastors of the Church may be very watchful in this matter, so that no scope may be given to Satan, whose chief aim it has always been to sow cockle amongst the wheat. There are some fanatics who have grown crazy enough to practise superstition and idolatry instead of the true cult, and to forget all proper limits, in respect both of God and of Mary.[1]

Fries goes on to cite Cardinal Newman, Otto Semmelroth and finally Otto Karrer:

> What a world of difference lies between that reverent love for the Mother of Christ which we find in early Christianity and the in many ways intolerable exaggerations of the Madonna-cult, especially in Latin countries, characterized as it is by a spiritual rhetoric which is fantasy run riot and by an emotionally extravagant popular sentimental attachment, with a corresponding lack of any theocentric or Christocentric orientation of life![2]

[1] Fries, *Antwort*, p. 140.
[2] Fries, *Antwort*, p. 141.

Protestants can, then, be sure that we too realize the dangers, and this not only in northern countries. No pleasure is taken at Rome in the mounting number of reports of apparitions, and the pseudo-apparitions at Heroldsbach are enough to show that the authorities are prepared to act. It is an extremely well-informed source which tells us that "on the subject of the titles of 'mediatrix' and 'co-redemptrix', Pius XII, a few weeks before his death and just after the Mariological Congress at Lourdes, said that both matters were too unclear and too unripe; that he had consciously and deliberately, throughout his pontificate, avoided taking up any positive attitude towards them, preferring to leave them to free theological discussion. It was not his intention to alter this attitude."[1] And Cardinal Montini, addressing the Liturgical Study Week at Vicenza, said:

> The liturgy is not only a means of teaching us dogmatic truth; it is also a school of holiness and one of the principle means of uniting our souls with Christ. Hence it is to be hoped that the work of this Congress will be devoted especially to this aspect of Marian liturgy. This will, where necessary, bring devotion to the most blessed Virgin back to its pure goal, so that it recovers its real function of bringing

[1] R. Leiber, S.J., writing on Pius XII in *Stimmen der Zeit*, reprinted in *Civitas*, 14 (1958), 81.

souls to Jesus by the speediest, most total and most loving transformation possible of the old man into the new man of righteousness and Christian holiness. Any other form of Marian piety, insufficiently orientated in this direction, would thereby necessarily show itself as deficient and as displeasing to the heavenly Mother.[1]

This, then, in the cause of reunion, is our Catholic task with reference to Marian devotion: the preservation of the right proportions, as laid down by Scripture, and the centring of all Marian devotion and Mariology upon Christ (not only as a verbally accepted principle, but thoroughly, in practice). Let us be understanding of Protestant difficulties over the new Marian dogmas; there is still much work to be done on deepening and rounding out the theological and especially the scriptural basis of these dogmas. But even in Mariology and Marian devotion, *peccatum per excessum*, the sin of excess, is not the only possible one; there is a *peccatum per defectum*, a sin by neglect, as well. And as we do not spare ourselves in our examination of conscience, so our Protestant brethren cannot spare themselves either; they must ask themselves some such questions as these: What do we make of the numerous Marian passages in

[1] Quoted by H. Schütte, *Um die Wiedervereinigung*, p. 148.

Scripture? Something positive and creative in theology and in piety, or only something critical and defensive? Where do we stand in regard to Luther's undeniable Marian piety? Can we really describe anti-Marianism as a requirement of "reform"? What are the roots of the anti-Marianism in *modern* Protestantism? Is it ultimately anti-Roman? Are Protestant Christians included or not in "All generations shall call me blessed?" Is calling her blessed to be done only silently, only shamefacedly, only peripherally, only privately? Is it only to be taught (and often not even that), or to be lived as well? Can we raise our voices in praise of Christ without also raising them in praise of her who spoke the decisive *fiat* to Christ? Can we be Christian without—though in a different way—being Marian too? Can we work at Christian theology without—though in a different way—working at Marian theology too? Considering how often it took centuries to plumb the depths of scriptural meaning, is it not possible that here too there were precious treasures lying hidden for quiet meditation and prayer to discover? Can there, finally, be any reunion in Christ which would leave the mystery of Mary to one side? Do we not here again need the undiminished Gospel, given its undiminished value and brought out into the full light of day?

Once again, it is only reform from *both* sides that can help us.

8. THE CHIEF OBSTACLE TO REUNION

The chief difficulty in the way of reunion lies in the two different concepts of the Church, and especially of the concrete organizational structure of the Church. We could, no doubt, reach agreement on many fundamental, dogmatic statements about the nature of the Church: the Church is the new People of God, founded and constituted by Christ upon the Prophets and Apostles; the one, holy, catholic and apostolic community of believers in Christ; the Bride of Jesus Christ and his at once visible and invisible body animated by his Spirit, and displaying at one and the same time a mysterious reality recognizable only to faith and an external juridical form. We might reach agreement not only in words but on their meaning, until we came to the question (which nevertheless determines the sense of all these expressions) of the Church's concrete organizational structure. And this is in no sense a purely external question; here are rooted all our still unresolved problems about the binding nature of ecclesiastical tradition, the structure and meaning of the sacraments (especially the Eucharist, private confession and priestly ordination), and the development of Mariology (the "new" dogmas of the immaculate conception of Mary and her assumption into heaven).

Ultimately, all questions about the concrete

organizational structure of the Church are crystallized in the question of *ecclesiastical office* (which includes the question of the "non-officials", the laity). The question has to be asked about every level of ecclesiastical office (the Petrine office, bishops, priests, deacons): what is their origin and nature? Whence do they receive their powers? What meaning and authority do they have in the domain of doctrine and dogma, of liturgy, of jurisdiction? In what concrete forms have they been put into operation and worked out in history?

Innumerable questions arise here, and they are particularly ticklish questions because they are not purely theoretical and dogmatic but practical and existential. We have reached the central challenge of the Reformation. True, the doctrine of justification was the theological lever which started Luther's own development as a reformer and then, in his hands, set the whole Reformation movement going and kept it going; and it was also the standard by which he measured every condition of things, good and bad, in the Church's life. But the central demand of the reformer was reformation: reform of the Church in head and members, reform of doctrine, of cult, of the people, of the Hierarchy at every level. Luther did not want to found a new Church but to reform the old, though it is true his concept of the Church was corrective rather than merely regulative in character.

7*

Hence it came about that Luther, who affirmed
the reality of ecclesiastical office, came into tragic
conflict with ecclesiastical office, and especially
with the office of Peter. This conflict was not
settled by excommunicating him; that was
barely the beginning. It has lasted throughout
all these centuries of schism. The *practical* opposition to ecclesiastical office, born of the pressures
and compulsions of that historical situation,
developed into an opposition *in principle,*
directed especially against the Petrine office. The
way was to some extent prepared for this opposition in principle by the unclear ecclesiology of
Luther and of the age; Luther himself based it
chiefly on his doctrine of justification, and the
German princes, in pursuit of their own ends
(an episcopate subject to themselves) carried it
out on the political level. But without the appalling conditions of ecclesiastical office, and especially that of Peter, at the end of the Middle
Ages, which called the opposition into being at
the practical level, its erection into a principle
would never have been achieved.

Today, we are trying, on both sides, to make
good the omissions of that time.[1] In the Catholic

[1] Cf. Otto Karrer's account of the present theological
position in his article on the apostolic succession and
the primacy in *Fragen der Theologie heute,* Einsiedeln,
1957, pp. 175–90; and, besides the bibliography there
given, K. H. Schelkle, *Jüngerschaft und Apostelamt,*
Freiburg, 1957; and O. Semmelroth, *Das geistliche Amt,*
Frankfurt, 1958.

Church efforts have been and are being made at a proper theological and practical valuation of the laity and the congregation in the Church; at a practical reform of ecclesiastical offices; at a theological explanation of the apostolic succession—not in an external sense (as though the conferring of office by ordination were an almost automatic mechanism) but in a spiritualized sense (the apostolic succession as the outward sign, presupposing faith, of the free activity of the Holy Spirit, who is the source of all gifts and powers). The Scripture significantly uses for ecclesiastical office not the words *arche* and *exousia* ("office" in the sense of "power") which were current in the secular domain, but *diakonia* ("service"). Ecclesiastical office is now being seen primarily not so much as authority but rather as service; service of the Gospel, to the measure and pattern of the Gospel; and so not as an autonomous institution but one bound to the risen Lord and his Holy Spirit for the benefit and blessing of the faithful. The man who holds office cannot then regard himself as "in command" of his office; rather he is bound to exercise it as service, in a spirit of humility and love; what is required of him in everything, great and small, is not a sense of dominion but a sense of service.

On the other hand, there is today a growing number of Protestant theologians (except for those who eliminate all the "Catholic" Scripture texts on a basis of subjective prejudice or explaining-away, or say that they are theologically irrelevant, which calls in question the authority of Scripture itself) who are trying to pay serious attention once more to what the Scriptures have to say about ecclesiastical office, and to ask themselves: Is there not, in Scripture, an apostolic vocation, blessing and commissioning, which confers the Spirit and is associated with prayer and the laying-on of hands—in fact, ordination, effectively communicating the grace of office and making it lawful in the eyes of the congregation? An ordination which, according to Paul's intention, was to be continued? Is there not then a succession, not only in general in the apostolic faith and confession of faith, but in a special apostolic office, intended precisely for the safeguarding of that apostolic faith—an apostolic succession? Was there not even in the Apostolic Church a visible hierarchy of bishops, presbyters and deacons? Is the present-day organization of the Protestant Church scriptural? Is not the question "By what authority?" a deeply disturbing question for many who hold office in the Protestant Church today? Is not some continuity of the powers of office needed, precisely in the sense of a succession? Does not even the *Confessio Augustana* recognize that the bishop holds office "by divine right"?

But the heart of the matter of ecclesiastical office, the great stone of stumbling, is the Petrine office. The question, "Do we need a Pope?" is the key question for reunion. A negative answer to it seems often to be the one and only thing which unites Protestants of completely different denominations, and which to a great extent they will not even discuss.

Nevertheless, there has been a change even here. The Papacy is recognized today by world public opinion as a moral force, and recent Popes have won the sympathy even of much of the non-Catholic world. It was not only Catholics who mourned at the death of Pius XII; tension over the papal election was not confined to Catholics, nor were they the only ones to rejoice at the election of John XXIII. In theology, too, there is more objective consideration nowadays, on the Protestant side, of the question of the Papacy: books like Oscar Cullmann's[1] represent an enormous advance in clarification. The problem today is not so much concerned with the really very striking scriptural testimony to the primacy of Peter (are the promise of the primacy in Matt. 16.18 and the conferring of it in John 21.15 ff. authentic—and did Peter exercise a primacy?) as with the primacy of the *Pope*: must the Petrine office necessarily have

[1] O. Cullmann, *Peter: Disciple—Apostle—Martyr*, London, 1953.

continued in the post-apostolic Church? Catholic theologians are trying to demonstrate the necessity of a Petrine office in the modern Church not on a merely sociological basis as expedient for the preservation of unity (though this unity as displayed by the Catholic Church is something of which Protestants, even when critical, often painfully feel their own lack) but theologically, by a more profound insight into the Old and New Testaments and early Christian tradition (there is a Petrine office, not because things would not work without it but because Christ willed it so). We are aiming, in ecclesiology, not at simply deducing the Church from the Papacy but at understanding the Papacy from the point of view of the Church. The Petrine office is understood primarily as a service, and *hence* as a supreme authority (authority not simply *over* the Church, but *in* the Church); the *primatus iurisdictionis* as springing from the *primatus fidei* (Luke 22.32); the Petrine office as Christ's own provision of a final court of arbitration and mediation in the service of unity.[1]

[1] Cf. e.g. (besides works of direct exegesis) O. Karrer, *Um die Einheit der Christen. Die Petrusfrage*, Frankfurt, 1953, and "Apostolische Nachfolge und Primat", also "Das Petrusamt in der Frühkirche", in *Festschrift J. Lortz*, Baden-Baden, 1957, 507–25; R. Grosche and H. Asmussen, *Brauchen wir einen Papst? Ein Gespräch zwischen den Konfessionen*, Cologne and Olten, 1957.

But what we said before of ecclesiastical office in general needs to be said even more emphatically of the Petrine office in particular, for this is a decisive factor in the discussion; Luther's denial of the Petrine office (for which his theology prepared the way, but which it did not make inevitable) did not fundamentally have a theoretical, exegetical or historical basis but was due to practical, existential forces at work in the situation at that time. Luther's opposition to the Pope did not begin from some new interpretation of Matt. 16.18 or John 21; the new exegetical and historical interpretation was a *consequence* of Luther's opposition to the Pope; and the opposition itself has to be explained in terms of the situation of Luther, of the Church at that time and the politics of that time, especially by the obscuring of the idea of the primacy by abuses in the Curia and by the Conciliar Movement. The *concrete situation* of the Papacy at that time made it impossible to see the *nature* of the Papacy clearly—and this is why the Papacy was denied. But it is equally true that all our exegetical and historical researches and discussions on the question *today*, all our theological reflexions *today* on the necessity and significance of the Petrine office in the post-apostolic Church, are essentially modified (and, as far as Protestants are concerned, hampered) by the concrete situation of the Papacy *today*.

In the interests of reunion, it is important that Catholics should see this question in all its concrete reality. It is not simply a matter of the pure essence but of the concrete historical actuality of the Petrine office. What are these concrete matters of which the Papacy still, in its essence, stands accused in Protestant eyes, and of which Catholics need to be aware? We are going to cite some examples deliberately chosen from Protestant theologians who are not exactly renowned for extreme anti-Catholicism, but are, on the contrary, frequently under fire for their "Catholicizing tendencies":

The Roman Church points to the division and disintegration in the Churches separated from her, at the existence of arbitrariness and confusion, at a disciplinary framework which does indubitably, however conscientious and ready to obey men may subjectively be, leave far too much scope to human self-assurance and obstinacy, and which simply does not admit of any effective counter-action to limit these destructive tendencies. The separated Churches point, no less convincingly, to the absolutist, centralist, indeed in some respects totalitarian features in the papal Church, where all too many men are afraid, and need to be afraid, of making the thoroughness of their Catholicism suspect by taking any stand against anything that comes from a higher level; where the freedom of the *pneuma hagion* seems to be localized in one spot, and the demand for a *sacrificium intellectus* is an ever-present threat.[1]

Our second Protestant witness:

We remember how many of the popes have been Italian or Roman popes; how difficult it has been for centuries, and how much more difficult it is obviously becoming in our own century, even to assert, let alone to maintain, anything, however Catholic, in the life of an individual local Church, whether dogmatic, liturgical or canonical, as against what Rome thinks, what Rome teaches, how Rome celebrates, how Rome judges. The age of the Reformation, the early Middle Ages, and the nineteenth and twentieth centuries, all provide an abundance of examples. It does not seem to depend on the character of individual popes or on the current level of religious life. The dominating factor must be a tendency to make a theological principle of subordinating what is Catholic to what is Roman, as to a spiritual, political, theological and juridical power; and this puts every area of the Catholic *oikoumene* into a kind of spiritual straitjacket. This Romanism and Roman centralism

[1] H. Dombois, "Der Kampf um das Kirchenrecht", in *Die Katholizität der Kirche*, Stuttgart, 1957, 296.

lay heavy during the later Middle Ages on
peoples, princes and, finally, the Reformers,
in the shape of financial and canonical dealings (the sale of indulgences!). Since then it
has—it seems to us—taken a much more definite and solid form, a Romanism which is
both canonical (with the codification and
application of the *Codex Juris Canonici*) and
theological in character. Roman theology,
Roman thought, Roman authorities take pre-
cedence when any Catholic decision has to be
reached on discipline, on law, and equally on
liturgy and theology. The framing-together
and growth of the "Catholic" Temple of God
seems to be more and more the work of a
merely human—*Roman* Catholic—technical
system rather than the framing together of
individual units into a single structure by
Christ the Cornerstone. What we are trying
to point out is something that has been developing for centuries (since long before the
Reformation)—a Roman "technique" in
liturgy, law and dogma, applied to the construction and maintenance of a "Catholic"
Church, which in fact actually *hinders* the
growth of the one Catholic body *in Christo*.
Without this "Roman technique", the tragedy
of the Reformation could never have pro-
gressed to such extremes. Anyone with any
knowledge of the historical sources must

realize this. Hence we cannot but give judgment even today in favour of the Reformers' protest on behalf of catholicity against the overweening *romanitas* of the Church, as something both Christian and Catholic.[1]

And our third Protestant witness:

If I agree that Peter received a special commission from the Lord—which seems to me to be certain; if, looking beyond that, it seems to me that the connecting link between Peter and the popes is insufficiently clearly visible; then it is, in addition, borne in upon me that in the course of development since then, especially in the last hundred years, things have appeared as part of the Papacy which I cannot reconcile with the New Testament. How do our Catholic brothers explain these things? This is the substance of my question. To me, it seems that one of the most thrilling things that we can observe in the New Testament is that, without any special reflection on the matter, exactly the same name is used for the individual community and for the worldwide Church. This can only mean that the individual diocese is in the full sense the Church, and at the same time that it cannot do without the totality of the Church. The

[1] M. Lackmann, "Ruf der evangelischen Christenheit zur katholischen Erfüllung", in *Katholische Reformation*, Stuttgart, 1958, 97–9.

same laws apply to both. So much is this so,
that it is impossible to deduce from the New
Testament any one single pattern of community life and discipline that applies to all
communities. The early Christian community,
then, is not centralist. Such ordinances as we
can find in the New Testament originating
from above the level of the local community
aim at allowing each individual diocese to
develop in its own freedom and independence,
rather than at hampering it and keeping it in
leading-strings. At the Council of Jerusalem
we find strong emphasis laid on what the
many had to say. The Bible is not in the least
ashamed to say that within the apostolic group
itself there were considerable disputes. And
what finally issues from this first Council is a
resolution to whose emergence the Apostles,
the presbyters and the whole community have
contributed. If this is the portrait of the young
Christian community as sketched in the New
Testament, it seems to me that it is so because
redemption includes the raising up of a personality capable, in itself, of judgement, as
was said of old by the prophet: "They shall
all be taught of God." It is this pattern that I
see threatened by the Catholic Church as she
is today. We see decisions of bishops annulled
by the Vatican without reference to the feelings of the bishop concerned. I do not need

to particularize, because these things are well known. At the Catholic Congress at Cologne, a Dutchwoman, Marga Klompé, pointed out the dangers of Vatican centralization with the utmost clarity, and appealed for self-determination for parishes, dioceses and provinces within the Church. I do not know whether there are papal honours that can be granted to women. But, as a Lutheran pastor, I hope that all who bear office are clear about this: this lady did the Vatican far greater service than any that could have been rendered by some enthusiast extolling its authority.

I am perfectly clear about the dangers that arise when people confuse Christian self-determination within the Church with the freedom of democracy. This is brought home to me every day by the misunderstanding of freedom in my own Church. But what I am not clear about is whether Catholics realize that every exaggeration of centralism on their part justifies our misunderstanding of freedom. For we are already, today, to such an extent all together in *one* boat that what anyone does affects all the others. It is because I am convinced that the lack of discipline in Protestantism is a grave blemish in it, so that it is in urgent need of consolidation, that I dare put to the Catholic Church the question whether centralism has not been carried too far, so that it is now having the opposite effect to what it was meant to have. For it is driving men away.

How has it come about that in Protestant circles the Vatican has the reputation of stifling all independence? I can well believe that malicious propaganda has contributed a great deal to it. Such propaganda did not start only yesterday, nor with the *Kulturkampf*. I have no hesitation in admitting that we have much to make good here which had its origin in ill-will or ignorance. But I would consider it historically untruthful if anyone tried to explain this reputation of the Vatican simply and solely on the basis of malicious or ignorant propaganda. A reputation of this sort can never arise without some sort of colour for it, coming in this case from the Pope himself. I should be glad to have a clearer insight in this matter than I have had hitherto.

Am I asking too much of our Catholic brothers when I beg them to tell us that our impression is unfounded, and to tell us in such a way that we can understand and be assured? For if we only could believe, if we could only be made to believe, that in the Catholic Church the independence of the individual congregation and diocese, in the New Testament sense, is guaranteed, and that the voice of the many who are all taught of

God is heard and respected, then we should, at least at the level of feeling, be in an entirely new situation. We should be a great step nearer to the unity of Christendom. I can only testify that the number of those in our ranks who would rejoice over such an outcome is very great.[1]

Once more, these are Protestants who are making special efforts at a positive understanding of the Catholic Church and the Petrine office. The majority of Protestants would say the same things in much stronger terms; we do not need further quotations. It is then plain that doctrinal arguments (exegetical, historical, theological) against the Papacy go hand in hand with those existential objections which were, as a matter of fact, prior to them in the order of time; that they may also be really (if perhaps unconsciously) the primary ones is at least arguable. To quote Otto Karrer:

Whatever may be the case in God's eyes, in men's eyes the *idea* of the Petrine office suffers under the burden of the *history* of the Petrine office. In other words, the whole difficulty of the problem is not a theological difficulty but one of historical origin and psychological in its effects, namely, fear of what may be in store for anyone who entrusts himself to

[1] H. Asmussen, *Brauchen wir einen Papst?*, 33–8.

Peter II. Consequently it does not help much, necessary though it is, to justify this holy office out of Scripture and the early Church. The theology of the primacy strikes men as ideology, and fails to take effect, so long as there lurks, at the back of their minds, the spectre of that "other" who once tempted Jesus, with all the danger that this involves for Christian freedom.[1]

It is significant that even such a theologian as Karl Barth, who can certainly not be accused of "Catholicizing tendencies", and who has often and vigorously proclaimed his opposition to the Papacy, admits that it is impossible to establish *from the Gospel* any *radical* objection either to the concentration of the apostolic function in Peter or to the possibility of a primacy in the Church, which might even be that of Rome.[2] But the question is: Can the Popes make their gigantic claim to be the Vicars of Christ *credible* to the outsider? Can they justify it not only historically but *spiritually*? Can they, that is, bring forward not only "persuasive words of human wisdom" but the "showing of the Spirit and power" (1 Cor. 2.4), so as to show in word and deed, at the level of the Gospel, that they

[1] O. Karrer, *Um die Einheit der Christen,* Frankfurt, 1953, p. 216.
[2] Cf. K. Barth, *Church Dogmatics,* Edinburgh, 1936, Vol. 1, pp. 106–115.

are more than a series of venerable and, in some cases, outstanding men (such as any secular dynasty can, after all, produce) but really and truly the Vicars of Christ?

True, as a Catholic one can and must reply at this point that the primacy, too, is a matter of faith; that the Pope is indeed the Vicar of *Christ*, but only, after all, the *Vicar* of Christ; that Christ did not promise us outstanding human personalities or great theologians for primates; indeed that he himself chose, no doubt intentionally, not such an outstanding person as Paul (or John), who could far more easily have given "the showing of the Spirit and power", but that fundamentally very "ordinary" man Peter. One can, in short, as a Catholic, protest to the Protestant that he must not demand *too* much from the human element in the Papacy. But the ultimate question still remains: Can the Papacy justify itself not only historically but spiritually? Can the Protestant Christian who is a man of good will hear, from the Chair of Peter as it is today, the *voice of the Good Shepherd*? So it is not the structure of the apostolic Church and its Petrine primacy that is the primary problem for us; it is the Catholic Church of *today*, with the primacy as it is *today*, as it is worked out at this moment in history in terms of ecclesiastical leadership, ecclesiastical teaching, ecclesiastical politics.

We *Catholics* can hear that voice, and we give thanks to Christ, who is the Lord of our Church, that we can hear it: the voice of Christ through the voice of him who during the time of his absence is to shepherd the flock. But if there is ever to be unity over this most difficult of questions, the question of the Pope, then we Catholics must get to know and try to understand the questionings and doubts, the objections and difficulties that Protestants make against the primacy as it is today. And we must try on our side— once more in an honest attempt at self-criticism and self-reform—to do our best and utmost to enable not only ourselves, who are within the Church's walls, but the millions outside to hear the voice of the Good Shepherd. And all this, in the Pope's words, as "a gentle invitation to seek and to find that unity for which Jesus Christ so fervently besought his heavenly Father". What is called for on the Protestant side is to consider whether the words of Scripture about the abiding rock (Matt. 16.18), the guiding and ruling key-bearer of the Kingdom of Heaven (Matt. 16.19), the special possessor of the power of binding and loosing (Matt. 16.19), the means of confirming the faith of others (Luke 22.32) and the deputy shepherd over the whole of Christ's flock (John 21.15 ff.), need to be understood more deeply, more powerfully, and with more relevance to the present day, by Protestant Christians. To ask themselves whether the Apostolic

Church, united in Peter, was not meant to go on, with the Petrine office continuing along with the pastoral office of the Apostles, for the sake of the Church (so that what was once *laid* as a foundation would continue to *function* as a foundation); whether it might not be possible to view the history of the popes, for all the dubious matters in it, in a somewhat more cheerful and understanding light; whether much disputing and bitterness could not now be forgotten, allowing us to recognize, across the barrier of all that is human and all too human, something which does indeed seem to be not the mere work of men but the work of our common Lord, promised to us and protected for us by the Word of God.

What is needed, then, is for Protestants to hear the voice of the Good Shepherd. Now, this does not depend simply on the person of the Pope. But nor is it independent of it. If we now say something about this matter, it is not because all the great and real difficulties in the way of reunion can be solved at once by some "personal" argument, but because the example of John XXIII has shown how important it is what kind of personality holds the office of Peter. Even Protestants have noticed how Pope John is in fact striving to be this very thing: a *good shepherd*. On the very evening of his election day, when addressing those who had taken part in the Conclave (28 Oct. 1958), he prayed for

God's blessing on his "very humble office of shepherd".[1] If Protestants are to find the Pope not merely "impressive" (which even the great ones of this world can be) but truly lovable, then it is certainly not going to be because he confronts them as a powerful prince of the Church, or a skilled diplomatist, or a highly cultured intellectual aristocrat, or even a splendidly hieratic priestly figure. If they want to be reminded of anything, it is not of the stately High Priest of the Jews nor the magnificent Pontifex Maximus of the Romans—to neither of whom did Jesus himself or Peter bear any resemblance—but (remembering the scene of the washing of Peter's feet) of the servant of the servants of God, *servus servorum Dei*; in short, of the Good Shepherd as described in the Gospel, as lived, humbly and simply, by Jesus first and, humbly and simply, by Peter after him.

The Good Shepherd was the theme of the homily which the Pope, quite unexpectedly and against all tradition, preached at his coronation Mass:

Some hope to find in the Pope a skilled diplomat and statesman, others a scholar, an organizer of public life, or one whose mind is in touch with every form of modern progress without exception. Venerable brethren and beloved sons, they are none of them on the

[1] *Herder-Korrespondenz* (1959–60), p. 113.

right track, for their ideal of a Pope does not
at all correspond to the true idea. The new
Pope is in his entire life more like Joseph
the son of Jacob, who had his brothers,
stricken by grievous misfortune, brought before him and declared to them, full of love
and compassion: "I am Joseph, your brother."
[Gen. 45.4.] The new Pope has before his
mind, more than all else, that wonderful
Gospel picture which St. John gives, in the
words of the Saviour himself, of the Good
Shepherd [cf. John 10.1–21] . . .[1]

The Pope cannot avoid the special position in
which his office puts him, but everything depends on the spirit in which he undertakes it.
Pope John asked in that same homily for prayers
for his humility:

For the key to the divine economy and the
command which contains in itself all others
is given in these words of the Gospel: "Learn
of me, for I am meek and humble of heart."
[Matt. 11.29.] Meekness and humility are then
a great commandment. All of you on this
earth who are devout and "fervent in spirit"
[Rom. 12.11], we beg you to pray to God,
continually beseeching him for your Pope, so
that he may continue forever in this evangelical meekness and humility. We are sure

[1] *Herder-Korrespondenz* (1959–60), p. 116.

that the practice of this virtue will bring a rich return, and that if it did indeed become the attitude of the father of all the faithful, this would be of immeasurable value even in the realm of humanity's social and purely earthly affairs.[1]

At his solemn taking possession of the Lateran Basilica, the Pope said:

The great processions which used to accompany the newly-elected Pope along the way from the Vatican to the Lateran would no longer be understood today . . . The new Pope's entry here has lost the splendour of former times, but how much it has gained instead in terms of inner spiritual meaning! No longer do we see a prince having the signs of outward power presented to him: what we see today is a priest, a father, a shepherd. Ceremonies of this sort, celebrated in community, lead us on to mutual pardon, understanding and love. They give us courage to carry out our duties, and to respect the rights of others in harmony with the rights that we maintain for ourselves.[2]

Then, after he had appealed especially for the reading of Holy Scripture ("so that it may light up the road of life from earliest youth to utmost

[1] *Herder-Korrespondenz* (1959–60), p. 117.
[2] *Herder-Korrespondenz* (1959–60), p. 175.

old age") and for participation in the eucharistic meal, he ended by saying:

> This is what we wish to express from the
> very first day of our pontificate, and to present
> ourselves before the world as, above all, a
> shepherd. And we think we can tell, from the
> far-reaching echoes of our coronation-day
> words in St. Peter's, that we have been under-
> stood in a living sense.[1]

The Cardinal Primate of Spain, who had
issued a pastoral letter on the election of the
Pope, received from him the following brief
letter in his own hand:

> Most beloved Eminence: Thanks, thanks
> for your pastoral letter about the new Pope.
> May the Lord forgive you the over-abundant
> words of praise which you have lavished upon
> his lowly person, and may he help me to bear
> fruit upon the way to sanctity. Ever from my
> heart I greet and bless you in all affection.
> Ioannes Papa XXIII.[2]

And words were followed by deeds: unassuming and by that very fact sensational deeds.
People are talking about the "new style" of
John XXIII. He visits the sick in the Roman
hospitals, old priests in old people's homes, the

[1] *Herder-Korrespondenz* (1959–60), p. 176.
[2] *Herder-Korrespondenz* (1959–60), p. 322.

convicts in the great Regina Coeli prison, devotes his time to the simple and the poor. He cuts down audiences which were often concerned rather with those of worldly importance, and prohibits applause in St. Peter's. Here too, even on solemn occasions, he often dispenses with the *sedia gestatoria* and makes his way in and out quite simply on foot; indeed, one can come across him there, engaged in private prayer. Pope John loves the Dialogue Mass, with the whole people (including on solemn occasions the cardinals and the diplomatic corps) saying their responses to the priest out loud and praying the Lord's Prayer with him. Whenever he can, he himself gives the body of the Lord to the faithful. Every day, in the Cappella Paolina in the Vatican, he celebrates a Dialogue Mass in which numerous laypeople and clerics employed in the Vatican take part; and even on Christmas Day the Pope expressly chooses to have, not a solemn papal High Mass, but a Dialogue Mass. He also wants everyone to join in the singing of the Gregorian chant. On the Sundays of Lent he takes part in the liturgy of the Stations and the penitential processions. In former times the Pope used to appear on horseback and with a splendid retinue; for many centuries no Pope had taken part in these ceremonies at all (though they were the original papal lenten liturgy). Pope John simply takes part on foot, walking behind the cross, praying and singing aloud with those around him—a sight to which the Romans are wholly unaccustomed. In the same way again he celebrates the liturgy of Holy Week with the people, himself performing the symbolic washing of the feet on Maundy Thursday, and, on Good Friday, when he comes to the ancient petition for the "faithless Jews", omitting the word "faithless". Pope John does not deliver many formal addresses, but he loves, on every occasion that offers itself, to preach; and in his sermons he often hides his learning, keeping simply to the words of the Gospel. These are not symptoms of some sort of pietistic narrowness; on the contrary, the Pope displays great breadth of mind. He does not hesitate to set etiquette and tradition aside (the limitation of the cardinals to seventy, for instance); he busies himself with improving social conditions for the Vatican staff, constantly makes expeditions into the city, the Campagna, the little villages round Castel Gandolfo, talking informally to people and everywhere radiating a delightful humour, genuine kindliness, simple humanity and, above all, a vast unassuming humility.

Thus St. Peter's office of good shepherd is making itself unmistakably felt. And if even Protestants often show that a Pope of this kind impresses them, this is not because they find such things simply touching in a human way,

8 + C.A.R.

but because they recognize them as *evangelical*, springing from the Gospel.

These are hopeful omens for reunion, reunion even on that very question which is our chief obstacle to coming together. Of course, we do not want to exaggerate the significance of all this. There is still so much unevangelical pomp and Byzantinism remaining, people say, and the Pope alone is not Rome. We know that many Protestant objections are not against the Pope but against the thing we may call "the Vatican" (Pius X attempted to change many things which were, in part, the result of the former constitution of the Papal State). Many of those who make these objections are, of course, unaware of the sheer strength and survival power of what has grown up through history and represents a great tradition ("N'oubliez jamais que le Vatican est d'abord une cour!"). But we are at one with our Protestant brethren here; we do not think, either, that what has been described here is enough to make the voice of the Good Shepherd heard again even outside the Catholic Church. Nor does Pope John think so. He has summoned an Ecumenical Council.

5. THE ECUMENICAL COUNCIL AND REUNION

1. DISAPPOINTMENT OR FULFILMENT?

THE Council will be either the fulfilment of a great hope or else a great disappointment. The fulfilment of a *small* hope would—given the grave world situation and the needs of Christendom—be in fact a great disappointment. It is better not to nourish illusions. In the introduction to this book we said that it would not be possible for this next Council, considering the vast and manifold difficulties in the way of reunion, to be a "Reunion Council". Our hopes cannot go as far as that. But the question is, Will this Council busy itself with mere proclamations, apologetics and matters of secondary importance (like, for example, the fruitless Fifth Council of the Lateran), which would be a great disappointment; or will it, by a bold and energetic renewal of the Catholic Church, create the *necessary conditions* for reunion, which would be the fulfilment of a great hope, that of the Pope himself?

It is indeed the importance of the matter in hand which does not permit of the Pope's acting on his own but has impelled him to summon an

Ecumenical Council. In this sense an Ecumenical Council can achieve more than could be done by the Pope alone. As Dr. Lorenz Jaeger, Archbishop of Paderborn, has put it:

In order to appreciate the full significance of an ecumenical council, we must have a clear notion of the true character of the infallibility of the Pope and of the episcopate in union with him. This infallibility does not communicate any new revelation, and infallible dogmas are not inspired. It is, rather, simply an assistance by which God protects his Church and her head from error when an official decision is being made in matters of faith and morals. Normally, before any such decision can be taken there must be intellectual work at the human level—thought, study of sources, theological reflection. If the Pope acts alone to decide questions of faith or to introduce measures of reform, then this divine assistance will indeed protect him against any error in doctrine. But it is not necessarily the case that he will hit upon the best possible formulation of a doctrine, or that he will institute the most effective possible reforms, such as will be most beneficial in given circumstances. The co-operation of the episcopate gathered together in council will often bring to light points of view of which the Pope had not thought. The Council of Chalcedon offers a good example of this. In his letter to Flavian Pope Leo stated the mystery of God's becoming man, the Incarnation, as against both Monophysites and Nestorians, and the Fathers of the Council of Chalcedon solemnly accepted and subscribed to the letter. But some of the bishops of the Eastern Church found that certain expressions in the papal letter did not take enough account of the different terminology used in the East. They worked out a new formulation of the dogma, which, in contrast to the lavish rhetoric of the papal letter, took account briefly, accurately and precisely of Eastern terminology (of which little was known in the West and at Rome), and which eliminated all possibility of false interpretation by heretical teachers. The result was a masterpiece of clarity and precision which deprived the Monophysites of any chance of accusing the Council of Nestorianism.[1]

But are we to disguise the truth that there is considerable scepticism (especially among Catholic theologians) of any effective results from the next Council? Many reasons are offered for this scepticism; but in every case, there is a

[1] Archbishop Lorenz Jaeger, "Das ökumenische Konzil", in a special number of *Echo der Zeit*, June 1959; cf. the remarks of Cardinal Tardini, Papal Secretary of State, in the *Osservatore Romano*, 1 Nov. 1959.

contra for each *pro* which does at least offer some limitation to it:

(a) Public opinion in the Catholic Church is insufficiently prepared either for the Council or for reunion. There is too little ecumenical thinking, no sense of the necessity of radical reforms; the only idea is that of an unconditional "return" of the others. On the other hand, anti-Roman feeling in Protestant Christendom is by no means yet defeated, and they simply would not seriously want to make any advance towards us. Indeed, some Protestant reactions to the announcement of the Council clearly revealed a fear of any confrontation and a *horror concreti* about anything to do with reunion.

But—it can hardly be denied that the general atmosphere has changed decisively since the First World War. Ecumenical efforts in the last few decades, often in small groups of laymen and theologians, have not been fruitless. In the Protestant world, the World Council of Churches has had a definite effect in deepening and focusing the longing for unity. There are already several places where there is an "ecumenical collection" by Protestants for Catholics and by Catholics for Protestants. Attention is being drawn more and more to this central need of modern Christendom, in the press, on the radio, in religious writing. The stresses of the time have brought Christians together; the

World Wars; political totalitarianism; the falling-away from religious practice and Christian belief in Europe and America; the often infinitesimal advances being made in the Christian missions (Christian disunity is everywhere a hindrance of the first importance); the rapidly increasing number of mixed marriages, with the strains in the religious life of these couples and of their children. It has often been discovered that our difficulties in pastoral work are the same —and that it is better to solve them together. We know now that Christians can only successfully confront the atheistic materialism of both East and West if they do it together, that only together can they bring the Gospel to bear upon the great problems facing the world: peace, hunger, population problems, the place of woman and the family in modern society, nationalism in the newly-awakened peoples, problems of social and technical development, of education and culture. More and more even the rank and file on both sides are becoming aware of the evil results of schism, and longing for a cure; readiness to understand each other is growing steadily; even prejudice against the Papacy has shrunk to a significant degree, as was made plain especially at the death of Pius XII and the election of John XXIII. The new Pope's appeal for unity in connection with the Ecumenical Council did, all things considered, awaken an astonishingly positive echo—a sign of much latent longing for reunion. (Only compare the strongly negative reaction of the whole non-Catholic world to the summoning of the Vatican Council by Pius IX!)

(b) Or it is said: Even if the people are longing for unity, the theologians are sure to make it impossible.

But—it is precisely among the leading theologians that there is a great readiness for understanding. We really want to get to know each other again, not according to inherited notions and prejudices but as we really are. Catholics are speaking to Protestant and Protestant to Catholic audiences. The theological, and especially the exegetical, works of the other side are being eagerly studied. What used to be "controversial" theology has today been largely transformed into a theology of encounter, a means of understanding, as is exemplified in numerous books. On the Protestant side, the progress of the biblical, liturgical, patristic, pastoral and social renewal of the Catholic Church is followed with the greatest interest. For a long time there have been, in Germany, regular meetings between Protestant and Catholic university professors. There have, also for a long time, been contacts between Anglican and Catholic theologians, and, more recently, between Catholic theologians and representatives of the Episcopalian Church in the United States. Most important of all, relations have for a long while been maintained between Catholic theologians and leading representatives of the World Council of Churches at Geneva, which have been intensified in connection with the Council but still have many heavy trials to undergo.

(c) Another objection: A gathering of all the bishops of the world will be too big and clumsy for fruitful discussion (the Church has at this time more than two thousand bishops and those of equivalent rank; to these, according to present canon law, must be added the heads of Orders, etc.; and two thousand seven hundred have been asked as expert advisers). It is hardly likely that procedural techniques and language will be adapted to modern requirements (as, e.g., in the United Nations, with synchronized multilingual translation); for traditional reasons, the Latin language will doubtless be maintained, which will put the considerably larger number of bishops of non-Latin nationality in this Council at a disadvantage in the discussions, and which is not an appropriate language either to the Orthodox or to Protestants.

But—Catholic voices have already been raised in favour of the use of modern languages and modern techniques in the discussions, and maintaining that the terminological difficulties of a

8*

theology which has long since ceased to be homo-
geneously Latin and become multilingual can
perfectly well be solved, as they easily are in the
fields of the secular sciences, law and politics.
It is also to be hoped that the difficulties arising
from having discussions in too large a unit are
recognized and will be dealt with. Even at the
Vatican Council, thanks to the lessons learnt at
Trent, great emphasis was laid on the work of
the preparatory commissions. The sorry experiences of the Vatican Council (with its huge mass
of schemata and decrees that came to nothing)
once more call for even more intensive preparatory work. This makes the preparatory commissions of decisive importance in many ways.
Hence it is important that they should not be of
onesided composition and so come, in advance,
to onesided conclusions, but that the various
tendencies in the whole episcopate, and so in
the whole Church, should be expressed in them.
Here too there are lessons to be learnt from the
Vatican Council. Although the schemata and
decrees had been prepared in great detail, they
were not—as Rome had expected—dealt with
quickly by the bishops; on the contrary, they
were violently torn to pieces, so that despite
months of work only a minimum of the tasks
undertaken were actually carried out. A
balanced composition of the commissions, imag-
ing the many sides of the world episcopate (and

its theologians), together with frank and realistic discussion when the commissions meet, could prevent much disappointment when it comes to the Council itself.

(d) It is also said: The majority of bishops and theologians come from "Latin" countries (Italy, Spain, Portugal, South and Central America) where Protestant Christianity is known almost exclusively in its negative aspects and by the unattractive missionary activities of American sects; hence they cannot, understandably, contribute much in the way of knowledge of controversial theology or deep understanding of the demands of Protestant Christianity. This would also affect, for understandable historical reasons, the Irish and so perhaps the North Americans (the memory of English oppression of Irish Catholics) and also the Poles (with their similar memories of the Prussians). The bishops from the countries where the Reformation began (Germany, Switzerland, Great Britain, the Netherlands, Scandinavia, etc.) are, on account of the method of voting used at Trent and the Vatican (not by nations or patriarchates, but by individuals), at a serious disadvantage. There are, for example, twenty-six bishops for Germany, two hundred and ninety for Italy (the uniting of dioceses envisaged in the Lateran Treaty has barely been begun).

But—it would indeed be a mistake to belittle

this difficulty. True, the Council is not to be regarded as a parliament. The bishops do represent the communities they rule, but it is as successors of the Apostles that they have their power, not from their communities; they are not delegates. Besides which, the object of discussion and voting in the Council is not simply to arrive at a majority decision but to achieve, sooner or later, at least moral unanimity, as an expression of the mind of the whole Church on a matter of belief, binding and inviolable. This brings us to a surely justified hope that in matters relating to reunion the bishops from countries where Catholics and Protestants are mixed together (especially the German- and English-speaking lands, Holland and France), who have a special moral authority to speak on these questions, will not be ignored. It is in any case permissible to doubt whether plenary sessions of the Council would be the best forum for unravelling highly complex and involved questions of controversy. This is something which undoubtedly calls both for a great deal of time and for very small discussion groups of highly qualified people, with experience of ecumenical work and exceptional knowledge both of Catholic and of Protestant doctrine. Hence it might be that the direct work of clarifying theological issues would be more appropriately done in inter-confessional theological commissions, such

as have been envisaged in various forms. This
does not, of course, exclude the possibility either
of private inter-confessional discussions or of
official inter-confessional consultations at the
Council; on the contrary, invitations to competent spokesmen of both the Orthodox and
Protestant Churches, who could give the Council their views on important matters relating to
reunion, would be extremely useful. At the same
time, personal contacts outside the Council could
be increased, and above all the commissions in
question could be given the official sanction of
the Church's highest authorities. Indeed, a
Roman Congregation for ecumenical matters,
with a competent team of advisers, to co-ordinate
the various fruitful initiatives that are being
made and to provide authentic information,
would be of the greatest value. The establishment of such a congregation, if it saw its task
not merely as negative supervision but as positive stimulation of efforts for unity, might be as
epoch-making an event in the cause of reunion
as the establishment of the Congregation *De
Propaganda Fide* was for the missions.

(e) One final objection: Certain circles in the
Catholic Church are not in the least interested
in the Council, and have no use for reform; it
would never be possible to get a majority in
favour of far-reaching changes. The Council
will be an external demonstration, a splendid

gathering of prelates, with everything that comes before it strained through carefully selected commissions and the whole business proceeding not so much according to the will of the bishops as that of the Pope. Before the Vatican Council too there was enthusiasm for reform and plans for reform, but not one single one of them was realized. Nor have the various reunion Councils in Church history had any permanent result.

But—we have already said something of how important it is that the commissions should function well. As for earlier reunion Councils, they were summoned less for pastoral than for political reasons. We should only have an equivalent situation today if fear of Communism were our principal motive for reunion. The experiences of the Vatican Council might, as we have suggested, lead just as well to positive as to negative results. Things that were never discussed then (only partly because of the early break-up of the Council) may well be discussed at the next Council. We may also remember that the standing orders proposed to the Vatican Council by Pius IX, which reserved to the Pope not only matters of general leadership and decision but the direction of everything down to the smallest detail, were set aside because of the objections of some of the bishops. An Ecumenical Council, by its very nature, serves not merely to advise the Pope but to decide matters in union with him. And John XXIII, to judge by the whole cast and fashion of his character and his way of exercising office, would be anything but the man to interfere autocratically in the deliberations of the Council. The next Council will be meeting in a completely different atmosphere from that of the Vatican Council (Pius IX's invitation to the Orthodox and his message to the Protestants could have no success in the atmosphere of that time; though well-meant, they were clumsily expressed). This Council does not have negative objects in view (such as defence against the errors of the time, whose condemnation by the Church is already well known, so that reiteration of it could scarcely make much impression on the world), but—according to the intention of John XXIII—the positive task of renewing the Church with the goal of reunion in view.

Such then are the pros and contras, both one-sided, neither without truth. No theologian can allay scepticism about the Council with words; only the Council can do it—with deeds. And here we have good hope. There is endless good will in the Church in our day, both among the Church's leaders and among her people. It would be too great a disappointment, for the Church and for the world, if nothing decisive were to come of it.

Isn't the Church too late? The question was

asked by some students, quite recently, as we were discussing together the great possibilities for the Church today in connection with the Council and reunion. Isn't a renewal for the sake of reunion already too late? Hasn't the falling-away from religion in Europe and America gone too far already? Haven't we failed in our missions to Islam? Has not the Chinese Rites Dispute meant that the favourable moment for evangelizing India, China and Japan has gone for good? Hasn't Communism—which has always been given its chance in Christian countries, by the failure of Christians—taken the place of Christianity in much of Europe and Asia? Isn't the Church too late?

It is a serious question; not in the sense of a preoccupation with results as measured by statistics, but in the sense of a conscientious self-questioning whether we Christians have not set up too many hindrances to the spread of the Gospel, and done too little that is positive. But does it make sense only to look sorrowfully backward? As if God our Lord were not still the hidden Lord of the world and its history, as if his Son had not redeemed the whole world and poured out his Spirit upon all peoples? We must look forward, and act not for a worldly victory of the Church but for the coming of the Kingdom of God.

This Council is taking place in an age when not only the earth but the moon and beyond are at stake; a transition period on an unprecedented scale, in which everything is being reset and readjusted—the beginning of a new age. From this arises our responsibility: responsibility in a tumultuous present for an unknown future. How will the Church look in the year 2000, or the year 2500? Are we going to have the courage for risks and experiments? Or are we going to be content with the cheap and narrow formula that we must let everything "grow"—not in the scriptural sense, but lazily and inactively letting things slide? Are our rectifications going to be too limited, our reforms too superficial, all our actions ultimately ineffectual?

The Pope has shown that we cannot simply let everything slide. Every great achievement in the Church's history has called for daring; not only patience, but initiative, not only prudence, but courage. All that has been said in this book so far is meant to show that we cannot make do with small actions; renewal today needs great ones. The Council cannot take us *all* the way, towards reunion or anything else. But if it is to be, not a great disappointment but the fulfilment of a great hope, then it is going to have to take us a *great* step forward.

2. POSSIBILITIES

It is not the task of a theologian to draw up a plan of renewal to be laid before the Council; it is not even his task to make proposals; all that is for the bishops. But there is something he can do to help; he can—and it is his duty to do it honestly—point out possibilities. It is then for the bishops to decide about these possibilities.

The concrete possibilities before the Council are innumerable; innumerable as the things that men would like to hope from the Church's leaders, innumerable as their desires for reform. Some such sorrowful litany as this, of widespread preoccupations and complaints on the part of Catholics, might be briefly recited: "Hopeless preaching and religious instruction—nonsense or rigidity in the liturgy—the Index—Roman centralism—episcopal bureaucracy—all the things wrong with the training of priests—convent and monastic education—political conformism—moral theology, specially on atom bombs and sex—Latin in the liturgy—scandals in the clergy—the fussing over organization and congresses in Catholic societies—Thomism — rationalism — Marianism — the pilgrimage racket . . ."

No serious and competent complaint is to be rejected outright and without proper examination. But if the Council is to achieve something more than mere discussion—actual deeds, and great deeds—then it is going to have to concentrate on a few essentials. What we can, according to the Pope's intention, exclude from the start are two things: (a) Further definition of traditionally controversional theological questions. The Pope himself, in his address to the Oriental College, said that it would today be impossible and fruitless to embark on endless discussions that would lead nowhere; we have pointed out above why it would be better, in the first instance, to conduct theological discussions of this sort elsewhere: (b) Further definition of Marian dogmas. John XXIII is even less likely than Pius XII to want to give dogmatic form to even more of Mariology. It is not only that his inaugural encyclical and his addresses on the work of the Council give an entirely different perspective. It is more fundamental than that. In the intention of the Pope, the Council is to prepare positively for reunion, and not to set up further barriers on the road to it. But a new Marian dogma would be regarded by separated Christians both in East and West as a new and considerable barrier to any rapprochement. It is extremely likely that any such definition would totally rob the Council of any possibility of bearing ecumenical fruit, bringing the accusation from separated Christians of both East and West that the Catholic Church is not honest in saying that she wants reunion; far from being wholly and primarily intent upon reunion, she builds up confessional differences to an even higher level—and this not in defence of some necessary dogma but for the sake of its development within the Church. Instead of being impelled by the thought of her co-responsibility for schism to reduce barriers to the lowest possible point, she is needlessly multiplying conditions for reunion.

These two limitations may serve to point us towards the positive possibilities of the Council —that inner renewal of the Church, in fact, which the Pope envisages as a preparation for reunion. But where are we to begin it? According to various things we have heard and various indications we have received, the Pope's intention is to begin with something of special importance for reunion: the restoration of its full value to the episcopal office.

There are two sets of reasons that suggest this. First, the way the present Pope has in various ways demonstrated his especial reverence for the episcopal office. John XXIII sees himself as essentially not just the supreme shepherd of the universal Church but as bishop of the diocese of Rome; hence his visits to the sick and the imprisoned, his numerous journeys into Rome and its environs, his participation in the liturgy of the Roman people, his summons of a Roman diocesan synod. But it is not only to the office of Bishop of Rome but to the episcopal office in general that he accords this special significance. It is perhaps not mere chance that in his letter to the Bishop of Trier he returned to the ancient scriptural and primitive usage and wrote of "the Church of Trier, and the other Churches, both in and outside your country".[1] The Conference of Italian Bishops, which has hitherto been entirely overshadowed in importance by the Pope and Curia, has thanks to him taken on a significance it has never had before. Not that the Pope gave any new formulation of the status of the bishops, but he encouraged them to better maintenance and use of those rights they already had. Even the resumption of the *tabella* audiences for the Curia, and the restriction of other audiences, may be reckoned as a "return to collegiate government of the Church's affairs":

Hence it has been made clear that private, special and group audiences will only be granted in entirely exceptional cases, since priority must be given to audiences for the College of Cardinals, *tabella* audiences for the Roman Curia, which deal with the most important needs of the Church, and audiences for bishops coming to Rome to make their visits *ad limina Apostolorum*.[2]

[1] *Herder-Korrespondenz* (1959–60), p. 459.
[2] *Herder-Korrespondenz* (1959–60), p. 466.

In public audiences, the Pope asks the bishops
—a most powerful symbolic gesture—not to receive his blessing but to join with him in giving
theirs. In this connection it is worth noting the
unusually strong emphasis laid on the divine
institution of the episcopate and the rights arising from this by Cardinal Tardini, Secretary of
State, in his Press conference on the Ecumenical
Council. He said that the Pope does not take the
place of the bishops in leading their dioceses;
the papal primacy cannot, by Christ's own institution, exclude the episcopate from the government of the Church; rather, the Pope is required
by Christ's own ordinance to accept the participation of the bishops in governing the Church;
and the summoning of an Ecumenical Council
must be understood in this light.[1]

Secondly, a proper examination of the episcopal office is suggested by the Vatican Council
itself, which has never been officially closed. It
is common knowledge that the Vatican Council
was originally to have discussed not merely a
schema on the primacy and infallibility of the
Pope but a vast schema "of the Church of
Christ", in which only chapters eleven and
twelve would treat of the Primacy (an appendix
on infallibility was added later), while chapters
one to ten would be on the Church in general
and chapters thirteen to fifteen on her relations

[1] *Osservatore Romano*, 1 Nov. 1959.

to secular authority. For reasons which we cannot go into here, all the chapters except those on the Pope were omitted. One of the most fundamental arguments of the minority of bishops against the definition of the primacy was that it was necessary to define the rights of the bishops first and only then to go on to define those of the Pope. But their voices did not prevail, and since developments in the political order then led to the break-up of the Council, the definition of the papal privileges remained as an unfinished torso, needing for its completion a definition of the rights of the episcopate, whose origin is just as much in Christ himself as the rights of the Petrine office. This completion would be today a work of quite immeasurable significance, not only for Protestants and Orthodox but also and primarily for the renewal of the Catholic Church herself, both in the traditional Catholic countries and in the missions.

It may be interesting in this connection to quote the "prophecy" that Cardinal Newman made, several times over, shortly after the Vatican Council, in 1871:

> But we must have a little faith. Abstract propositions avail little—theology surrounds them with a variety of limitations, explanations, etc. No truth stands by itself—each is kept in order and harmonized by other truths.

The dogmas relative to the Holy Trinity and the Incarnation were not struck off all at once —but piecemeal—one Council did one thing, another a second—and so the whole dogma was built up. And the first portion of it looked extreme—and controversies rose upon it— and these controversies led to the second, and third Councils, and they did not *reverse* the first, but *explained* and *completed* what was first done. So will it be now. Future popes will explain and in one sense limit their own power. This would be unlikely, if they acted merely as men, but God will overrule them. Pius has been overruled—I believe he wished a much more stringent dogma than he has got. Let us have faith and patience.[1]

. . . Let us have a little faith in her [the Church] I say. Pius is not the last of the popes. The fourth Council modified the third, the fifth the fourth . . . The late definition does not so much need to be undone, as to be completed . . . Let us be patient, let us have faith, and a new Pope, and a re-assembled Council may trim the boat.[2]

Some Protestant Christians (particularly those of Calvinist persuasion) may possibly think that

[1] Letter to Miss Holmes, in Wilfrid Ward, *The Life of John Henry Cardinal Newman*, London, 1913, vol. 2, p. 379.

[2] Letter to Plummer, in F. L. Cross, *John Henry Newman*, London, 1933, p. 170.

emphasis upon the episcopal office is not going to be any great advantage to the cause of reunion. But there is more to it than this; the episcopal office involves not only the personal office of the bishop but the whole of the local Church (diocese, country, continent) which the bishop embodies. Greater self-determination for the bishop means greater self-determination for the local Church. This means at once that this question is of fundamental importance for reunion with the Eastern Church, where the federal principle is so strongly emphasized. Orthodox theologians sometimes go so far as to maintain that the Latin Church has suppressed episcopacy and thus abandoned the apostolic order. But the significance of the local Church has also, ever since the Reformers, been a preoccupation of Protestants. Nor can it be ignored that in the World Council of Churches there is a growing number of voices, and important ones, being heard which attach great importance to the episcopal office; not only among the Anglicans and Swedish Lutherans, but many German Lutherans as well, and especially that experiment which is often pointed out, in circles connected with the World Council, as the very model of ecumenical work, the Church of South India. Developments in this direction must not be overlooked, always assuming that they do not stop short at untheological feelings about bishops but

involve a clearly thought-out scriptural theology
of the episcopal office. A restoration of the episcopal office to its full value within the Catholic
Church might—without damaging, but rather
nourishing unity—do much to limit that
"Roman centralism" (cf. our quotations from
Protestant witnesses) which is much feared by
Protestants and also deplored, in many of its
operations, by Catholic bishops. At the same
time, it would create the conditions (as we shall
shortly show) in which more of the demands
validly made by Protestants could be fulfilled;
and it would be, simultaneously, a strengthening of Church order and a clarification of the
structure of the Church in doctrine and in
practice.

But how, in practice, is the episcopal office to
be restored to its full value? It is pointed out,
rightly, in the Curia that the episcopal office
would be at once restored, to quite a significant
degree, if all the bishops would have sufficient
sense of responsibility to exercise *the rights they
already have*, fully and entirely, instead of
appealing to the Curia for answers and action
in cases where they could, as bishops, give the
answers and take the action themselves. This is
indeed a general problem, and a basic one, in
the ecclesiastical decentralization for which
Catholics often clamour; what is needed is the
courage to take responsibility at every level, in
bishops, priests and layfolk.

What is important is to preserve the personal character of the Church's community life, with the smaller communities (and those who hold office in them—in dioceses, Orders, parishes, Catholic societies) maintaining their own individual constitutional life and at the same time truly living it as part of the Church. If we look at it this way, there can only be as much centralism in the Church as we ourselves bring about. The protest against centralism often stands for a readiness simply to ignore the current norms of the Church's community life. It would be more to the point to cure any real abuses that may exist within one's own area of responsibility without waiting for higher authority to find itself compelled—because of the principle of subsidiarity—to interfere. If "self-help" of this sort were normal, higher authority would have no occasion to intervene. But experience shows that this does not often happen; indeed, that application is all too often made from below to higher authority, that those higher up are asked to introduce unpopular measures, and thus responsibility for them is transferred from below upward. Guarding against centralism means having the courage for personal responsibility, and so, primarily, the readiness to take odium on oneself and be unpopular. It is undoubtedly true that in an earlier age

of the Church there was no inclination to give
an immediate authoritative decision on every
doctrinal question that arose. How many
questions there were that were discussed for
centuries! Or authority itself would point to
the opinion of recognized authors as the
answer. So long as dangers to the religious
and moral life of the faithful do not arise, or
so long as, when they do arise, they can be
met by the authority immediately concerned,
there is no direct occasion for intervention
from a higher level.[1]

However, this still leaves room for considering
a more full-scale restoration in the framework
of the Ecumenical Council. How is this to come
about? Here again, we can do no more than
briefly sketch a few possibilities. To understand
what we mean by these possibilities it is important to realize that they are not "personal dis-
coveries" but hopes which are in the air at
present, as anyone will agree who has a knowledge of present problems in Catholic theology
and Catholic life. It was a great joy to me to
hear, from many competent sources, that a vivid
sense of the urgency of these hopes is shared by
alert minds not only in mixed Protestant-
Catholic countries like ours but in Rome, in the
Latin countries, and above all in our missions.

[1] W. Bertrams, S.J., "Das Subsidiaritätsprinzip in der
Kirche", in *Stimmen der Zeit*, 160 (1957), 264 ff.

For what follows it will be appropriate to distinguish between two closely related levels, those of dogmatic theory and of practical organization.

(1) The level of dogmatic theory. Even in the Vatican definition of the papal privileges a reference was included to the bishops: "Appointed by the Holy Spirit, and holding the place of the Apostles, they pasture and rule the flocks entrusted to them as true shepherds."[1] An outline for a further formulation of the doctrine of the episcopal office might well be provided by the declaration of the German bishops on the relation of bishops to the Pope, which was made against Bismarck and solemnly approved by Pius IX as an admirable interpretation of the Vatican Council. In this it is declared, on the negative side, that the Pope cannot alter the episcopal government of the Church as established by Christ; the bishops are not tools or officials of the Pope; their rights cannot be abrogated or absorbed by the Pope, nor papal authority substituted for their authority; the Pope is Bishop of Rome, not Bishop of Cologne or Breslau. On the positive side, it is declared that: the bishops are appointed by Christ as successors of the Apostles; the episcopate is just as much of divine institution as the papacy; this is the basis of its rights and its duties.

[1] Denzinger, *Enchiridion Symbolorum*, no. 1828.

This might be the starting point for, in particular, a more complete formulation of papal infallibility; the interrogation of the Church by
the Pope, as a preliminary to definition (already
stated in Denzinger, no. 1836), which was put
into practice in connection with both the Marian
dogmas, might be described in more precise and
imperative terms.[1] Starting from this, the whole
meaning of the episcopate as something that
cannot be superseded could be theologically
deepened, especially if full use were made of
exegetical and historical learning.

Of course, a definition of the episcopal office
would involve difficult theological problems that
have not yet been solved: a general theological
description of ecclesiastical office (which would
need to be explicitly defined as service, ministry

[1] Cf. Cardinal Tardini, in his Press conference about
the Council: "The real and only mainspring of papal
infallibility is divine assistance. But this does not confer
any kind of omniscience on the Pope; hence the Pope
is bound not to neglect any means of serious and
intelligent scholarly research, in order to reach his final
conclusion. Hence every papal definition rests upon a
considerable work of profound research into the divine
teaching, as contained in Scripture, in sacred tradition,
in the magisterium of the Church and in the belief of
the Christian people. And in this field it is opportune
to consult the bishops of the Catholic Church." Tardini
then spoke of the two recent Marian dogmas, concerning which the Pope virtually summoned an Ecumenical
Council without giving it the juridical form of one (see
the *Osservatore Romano*, 1 Nov. 1959).

—of the Word, of the sacraments, of charity—
with authority given for the sake of service, so
that service can be carried out); then the relation of the Primacy to the episcopate (or the
Council), the theological meaning of the *col-
legium episcoporum,* and the balanced interpretation of the Vatican Council's "ex sese, non
ex consensu Ecclesiae"); and finally the relation
of the episcopal to the priestly office (with special
reference to the sacrament of orders and to
jurisdiction), and the relation of the episcopal
office to the body of the faithful, etc. It is the
theologian's task, not merely to sit and wait for
the decision of the Council, which will not be
the recipient of any fresh revelation, but to
serve the Church by clarifying the matters in
hand as thoroughly as possible by exploring them
exegetically, dogmatically and historically before
the Council begins.[1] At the Council itself it then

[1] Recent work on the episcopal office: J. Colson,
L'Évêque dans les communautés primitives, Paris, 1951;
J. Lécuyer, "Aux origines de la théologie Thomiste de
l'épiscopat", in *Gregorianum,* 35 (1954), 56–89;
L'Évêque et son église (*Cahiers sur la Pierre-Qui-Vire,*
8), Geneva, 1955; B. Botte, "Presbyterium et Ordo
Episcoporum", in *Irénikon,* 29 (1956), 5–27; D. O.
Rousseau, "La Vraie Valeur de l'épiscopat dans l'Église
d'après des importants documents de 1875", in *Irénikon,*
29 (1956), 121–50; K. Rahner, "Primat und Episkopat",
in *Stimmen der Zeit,* 161 (1958), 321–36 (also in *Sendung und Gnade. Beiträge zur Pastoraltheologie,* Innsbruck, 1959, pp. 239–62).

becomes possible—according to the principle *in necessariis unitas, in dubiis libertas*—to leave very many questions, even perhaps most of them, open (as at Trent scholastic disputes were deliberately set aside in favour of the statement, preferably in scriptural terms, of necessary matters of faith).

The essential point is that the relation of bishops to Pope corresponds to the biblical relation of Apostles to Peter. We must curtail neither the rights of the Petrine office (which is conciliarism) nor the rights of the apostolic office (which is papalism). The unchangeable constitution of the Catholic Church, as founded by Christ and shown in prototype in the Acts of the Apostles, is at once Petrine and apostolic, at once hierarchical and collegiate. Hence the important thing is always the preservation of these features of the Church's structure, as displayed in the Acts and originating from Christ himself. For this reason it is a good thing always to keep the order of things in the apostolic Church before our mind's eye, not indeed as a model to be mechanically copied but as a determinative norm.

In his historical enquiry into the Petrine office in the early Church, Otto Karrer came, amongst other things, to the following conclusions:

> The idea of the Petrine office was there from the beginning. The Church was given

her structure in her very foundation by our
Lord. She did not sail under sealed orders,
not to be opened till later on in the voyage.
But the Petrine office is not the same as a
papalism capable of ignoring the divine rights
of the Church's universal episcopate; it is the
highest organ of arbitration, for the sake of
unity, and for this it was given by Christ and
is necessary. Hence the essential function of
the Petrine office asserts itself in cases of conflict for which the authority of the bishop in
his diocese or the patriarch in his province
does not suffice. Whenever the bishop's
authority is enough, there is at least no absolute need for the Petrine office to take a hand
. . . But a certain tension between episcopal
and Petrine tendencies, analogous to the tension between ecclesiastical authority and the
private conscience, is something immanent in
the Church and even a mark of vitality in the
Christian community. The Petrine office is
more in the nature of a breakwater against
errors than a fertile source of doctrine. It is
essentially regulative; but, as such, according
to our belief, it is willed by Christ and providential to such a degree that, in the light of
early Christian history, none of the most important of the traditional beliefs of Christendom—the canon of Scripture, Christology, the
dogmas concerning the Trinity, the validity
9+G.A.R.

of heretical baptism—is ultimately thinkable
without it.[1]

It will not occur, of course, to anyone to deny
that many developments in the Church's history
have been healthy. It is always foolish to try to
wipe out any development that has considerable
historical roots; the Reformers were too little
aware of this. It is obviously impossible simply
to copy the primitive Church in the modern
world. And, finally, who could fail to see the
historical necessity of a certain degree of centralization? It was necessary to ensure the independence of the Church in the Middle Ages, it
was necessary in face of anti-Church movements
and anti-Church states in modern times, and it
is still necessary today in a world which, on the
one hand, is one world as never before, thanks
to improved communications and technical
advances, and, on the other, exposes the security
and stability of thought and belief to so many
pressures. But unity is not sameness but the very
opposite. And it is more necessary than ever
today, both because of the nationalism of the
newly-awakened peoples and for many other
reasons rooted in the spiritual experiences of
modern man, not to allow Catholic unity to freeze
into uniformity, but to let it flower in manifold
variety. If we do not see this, then all our efforts

[1] O. Karrer, "Das Petrusamt in der Frühkirche", in
Festschrift, 524 f.

for reunion will be in vain; for while unity is
desired outside the Catholic Church as well as
inside, uniformity certainly is not. But even
within the Church it would be a great loss; for
it would mean that many valuable forces would,
without any necessity, remain fettered, and not
be able to develop. Finally, it would be to ignore
the ominous warning of the Iron Curtain, summoning us to realize in advance, and make our
preparations accordingly, that international conflicts in the modern world can cut off the episcopate of a very considerable area from Rome for
decades at a time.

(2) The level of practical organization. One
reason why a simple restoration of primitive
Church order is not possible is that a modern
diocese is no longer a relatively closed unit. The
world has shrunk, and dioceses have to be seen
in a larger national and international context.
The majority of important diocesan matters can
only be dealt with today at an interdiocesan
level. The national Bishops' Conferences (which
can give themselves the status of councils, so as
to have full legislative powers) have greatly increased in importance. They have been much
encouraged by Rome (e.g., in South America,
where a continental Bishops' Conference was set
up). For purposes of reorganization it would,
then, be better if a transfer of administrative
powers and initiative were made, not to the individual bishop but to the Bishops' Conference

of a country, a language-area or a continent. Indeed, in the early Church the diocese was embedded in the larger units of the metropolitan area and patriarchate. These larger units held an important position in the universal Church and, as intermediate levels of authority, had a determining influence on the life of the Church. A reconstruction of the old system of patriarchates, on the lines of a mere copy, would not be at all desirable; but what would be welcome would be a *renewal*, in accordance with the conditions of our own time, of a *corresponding* intermediate level in the Church, with the aid of the Bishops' Conferences. They could also, as and when necessary, be assisted by auxiliary bodies of an administrative or judicial nature, by standing or temporary commissions of experts, and by lay groups—all not in the cause of centralization but of decentralization.

A strengthening of these intermediate levels would certainly lead to a renewal throughout the Church. Pius XII expressly declared that the "principle of subsidiarity" applies to "social life in all its forms, and even to the life of the Church, though without compromising her hierarchical structure".[1] So let us give more and more thought to the enormous relevance of what Pius XI said in *Quadragesimo Anno* about this

[1] Pius XII, address to the newly appointed Cardinals, *Acta Apostolicae Sedis*, 38 (1946), 144 ff.

principle, which applies to every kind of human community:

It is indeed true, as history clearly proves, that owing to changed circumstances much that was formerly done by small groups can nowadays only be done by large associations. None the less, just as it is wrong to withdraw from the individual and commit to a group what private enterprise and industry can accomplish, so too it is an injustice, a grave evil and a disturbance of right order, for a larger and higher association to arrogate to itself functions which can be performed efficiently by smaller and lower societies. This is a fundamental principle of social philosophy, unshaken and unchangeable. Of its very nature the true aim of all social activity should be to help members of the social body, but never to destroy or absorb them.[1]

And what Pius XI says of the State can be applied, analogously, to the Church:

The State, therefore, would leave to smaller groups the settlement of business of minor importance, which otherwise would greatly distract it; it will thus carry out with greater freedom, power and success the tasks belonging to it alone, because it alone can effectively

[1] Pius XI, Encyclical *Quadragesimo Anno*, trans. as *The Social Order*, London, C.T.S., 1931, para. 79.

accomplish these; directing, watching, stimulating, restraining, as circumstances suggest
and necessity demands. Let those in power,
therefore, be convinced that the more faith-
fully this principle of subsidiary function be
followed, and a graded hierarchical order
exist between various associations, the greater
will be both social authority and social effi-
ciency, and the happier and more prosperous
the condition of the commonwealth.[1]

The degree to which the central authority
works through subordinate authorities; the
degree, that is, of decentralization and real self-
determination in smaller communities; the
degree to which the central authority is sparing
of direct intervention (as much freedom as
possible, as much intervention as *necessary*; the
nations with the most laws are not the happiest
ones)—these are the measures by which we can
tell how far the principle of subsidiarity is being
put into practice in a society.

Our Catholic Church would recover a far
greater similarity to the apostolic and early

[1] *Quadrigesimo Anno* (*The Social Order*), para. 80.
For the philosophical and theological basis of the prin-
ciple of subsidiarity, see W. Bertrams, S.J., "De Principio
Subsidiaritatis in Iure Canonico", in *Periodica de Re
Morali Canonica*, 46 (1957), 3–65; "Vom Sinn des Sub-
sidiaritätsgesetzes", in *Orientierung*, 21 (1957), 76–9;
and "Das Subsidiaritätsprinzip in der Kirche", in
Stimmen der Zeit, 160 (1957), 252–67.

Church if the Pope's desires in the matter of the principle of subsidiarity were seriously carried out. There would be an abundance of fruitful initiatives and developments in the Church at large if the episcopal office and the local Church (in a diocese, a country, a continent) became more important once again. Nor is it at all necessary to fear that some sort of federalist chaos would set in, for the weight of the central authority would still remain quite sufficiently great, and would have at its disposal every modern technique for control and intervention. The meaning of the Petrine office as a centre of unity in the Church, as against the errors of Jansenism, Gallicanism and Febronianism, has been worked out dogmatically with such clarity that there is no danger now of losing anything that is essentially Catholic. Our unity is, thank God, so firmly established that separatism is dead. And it is precisely this situation which calls for a loosening-up within our borders and makes it possible to carry it out. And here let us not forget that from the beginning the Church has had *two* principles of unity: the bond between the bishops and the See of Peter, and the bond *between the bishops themselves*. It is this *communion* between the bishops (which was maintained in various ways in the early Church) whose significance could be strengthened once more by better interrelations at the national and international levels between the bishops themselves, and not only between each one and the centre. And solidarity between the bishops of different nations would encourage a growth in solidarity between Christians and between nations, which is urgently necessary for so many reasons (not the least of which is world peace).

If this restoration of the full value of the episcopal office is really to further the renewal of the Church, and through that the cause of reunion, then it must not be of a merely proclamatory character or be limited to unimportant details. We know that even at the Vatican Council bishops were complaining that they, the holders of "ordinary jurisdiction", were required to apply to Rome for powers (renewable every five years) to deal with cases which are constantly recurring (marriage cases etc.). But to restore such powers as *these* to their "ordinary" holders, valuable though it would be in itself, would neither impress Protestants nor bring about that interior renewal of the Church which is the purpose of the Council. Reunion calls for something more fundamental. It calls, not indeed for revolutionary, but certainly for bold measures. It calls for the courage to restore to the bishops —whether as the episcopate of a country, or of a language area, or of a continent—their fundamental, original, ordinary episcopal powers, while preserving their relation to the Petrine office and its privileges and keeping within a suitable framework of universal law.

One concrete historical example will show how reform can be carried out much better and more easily by the bishops than by the central authority. As we know, the introduction of a universal catechism for the whole Church was proposed at the Vatican Council and discussed for a long time. Many of the bishops fought energetically against such an imposition of uniformity. The plan was at last abandoned. Since then it has been demonstrated, in Germany, that a reform of the catechism was indeed necessary, but that the episcopate, with the help of a committee of experts, could carry it out much more easily and appropriately. What could not be done by any universal catechism, intended equally for Africans and Eskimos, Americans and Japanese, Spaniards and Germans (whatever one may happen to think of Cardinal Bellarmine's catechism), has been done, in model fashion, by the German catechism. Freshly rooted both in Scripture and redemptive history, and in the best Catholic tradition, it also takes account of new pedagogical and didactic methods, and of new developments in theology, precisely as these affect *German*-speaking countries, and of the special conditions in education, culture, psychology and the Church itself, that are found *there*. The features that make this

9*

reform an excellent example are: (a) It was carried out within a general "framework of law" common to the whole Church (provided in this case by the creeds and the Church's doctrinal pronouncements, and controlled by the episcopate's referring back to Rome): (b) It was carried out not by a single bishop but by the episcopate of the whole country. This means that unity is preserved; sufficient personal and financial resources are available to keep a first-class committee of experts at work for a long time; and the bishops are in a position, because of their close and accurate knowledge of the situation, to carry out a reform in accordance with the real situation in their *own* country. This does not exclude the possibility that reforms of this sort may extend their influence beyond national frontiers; indeed, the German catechism has already been adopted outside Germany. Reform on these lines preserves the unity of the Church ("unity in essentials") and at the same time her Catholic variety ("freedom in inessentials"); it is not imposed from outside but grows organically out of the local Church; it does not—as is to some extent inevitable with universal reforms —have to remain unchanged for what may be an excessively long period, but can be easily adapted to meet a new situation. (Should we not have to wait for centuries before we achieve sufficient approximations between ourselves to make a *universal* catechism possible, and would not these approximations, once universally achieved, inevitably grow into "matters of principle"?)

It is worth considering whether this one case of the reform of the Catechism might not be a model for corresponding reforms of, for instance, the Mass, the Breviary, the law of marriage, etc., which would restore a fuller meaning to the episcopal office and at the same time accomplish a fundamental renewal of the Church with a view to ultimate reunion. The Vatican Council showed that a council cannot achieve any results in practical reforming measures, even by months of work, if it tries to go into details. What a council could do today, what would have a real meaning in the present situation, is to provide a *basic framework of law* within which the *bishops* of the various countries, language-areas or continents could, under the general direction and supervision of the Petrine office, carry out concrete reforms. This does not exclude the possibility of dealing with some problems, not with a strict framework of legislation but rather with general directives, perhaps in the form of a conciliar encyclical (e.g., to missionaries on missionary methods, to the Curia, etc.). In any case, we need in our present situation, which has changed in so many ways, to keep our minds open for new forms of conciliar work. (Perhaps, too, we could learn something from the methods of the World Council of Churches, which has been doing intensive work during the last few years under analogous difficulties and with a valuable accumulation of experience.)

It is a little risky to go further than this into concrete details about measures of renewal; some issues are too hot to handle. But it is a theologian's serious duty to the Church, and one which he must not shirk, to point out not only principles but actual courses of action, though of course still only in the sense of *possibilities* offered, with all deference, for discussion, their adoption and realization being entirely a matter for the bishops. What, then, are the concrete possibilities of enhancing the significance of the episcopal office at the practical, organizational level? What are the concrete possibilities for reforms which, at the same time as they restore its full value to the episcopal office, will be steps towards the renewal of the Church and hence towards reunion? We shall distinguish between the priestly, the pastoral and the teaching office of the bishop, and within this framework we suggest—of necessity briefly, cursorily, and without laying any extensive foundation— the following examples, which do not, of course, exhaust all the possibilities.

(a) Under the heading of the bishop's priestly office, the first example is the liturgy of the Mass.

The conciliar framework of legislation, concentrating with the utmost brevity and simplicity on *what* was to be done while leaving *how* it was to be done as wide open as possible, would lay down what absolutely must be manifested in each and every Catholic Mass-liturgy: first, a clearly and intelligibly constructed Service of the Word, with prayers, singing and reading of the Scriptures taken from the whole of the Old and New Testaments (perhaps even a complete reading, especially of the New Testament, covering all the days of the year), with at least a short homiletic instruction to complete it; then the preparation of the gifts with prayers of petition (and perhaps an offertory procession); then, at the centre, the eucharistic prayer (the "Canon", with the memorial of the Last Supper, somewhat on the model of the oldest of the Roman eucharistic prayers, that of Hippolytus), which should be intelligibly, simply and clearly constructed, but (as the prefaces are today) variable according to the season of the Church's year; and finally, the eucharistic meal and the dismissal. Such further regulations as seem absolutely necessary for the preservation of unity (as for instance the principal dates of the Church's year etc.) could be added.

Within a legislative framework of this sort, it would then be for the *episcopate* of a country, a language-area or a continent, to give concrete embodiment to the liturgical form of the Mass. The episcopate, with the help of a committee of experts (which would keep contact with their opposite numbers in other countries, a further organic means of preserving a certain unity), could solve the concrete difficulties facing the various countries and continents in their very different stages of advance in the liturgical revival: the vernacular (the most important current question); the arrangement of Scripture reading; concelebration; Communion under both kinds on special occasions; reduction, by combination, of the number of saints' days; the "high" and "low" forms of Mass; vestments, gestures, music, singing. And they could work out a basic form of the Mass which would, again, in various matters (chants, readings, prayers) leave some freedom on occasion to the individual priest. The rite thus worked out would then be submitted to the Pope for approval.

This manner of procedure would be similar to that of the reform of the German Catechism. This would provide a solution to the problem of rites, which is as important in traditional Christian countries as it is in the missions, and it would do it not in an archeologizing sense but in a truly Catholic fashion appropriate to our times, and without neglecting the demands of unity. At the same time, liturgical reform on these lines would make room for reunion with our separated brethren, to whom, in liturgical matters, wide liberty (in the form of a different "rite") could be allowed, within the bounds of fundamental unity. The Catholic Church herself could reap marvellous blessings from such a reform of the Mass. There would be a huge increase in the intelligibility and popular character of the Mass, in its potentiality to be deeply experienced and its power to illuminate (powers which have been hitherto to far too great an extent limited to popular "devotions"); there would be a concentration on what is essential to our faith, a new, active participation of the people as in the early days, and a deepening of their love for the Holy Scriptures, which would be read and explained to them in all their richness.[1]

[1] On the history of the Roman Mass, cf. J. A. Jungmann's definitive work, *The Mass of the Roman Rite: Its Origins and Development*, London, 1959. On current hopes for reform, the proceedings and conclusions of the various national and international liturgical congresses, and a mass of articles. The expression of these hopes has not, as yet, taken account of the far greater potentialities of an ecumenical council. That hopes in the missions are largely the same as those in the traditionally Christian countries is shown by the work of J. Hofinger and J. Kellner, *Liturgische Erneuerung in der Weltmission*, Innsbruck, 1957. For the way in which the reform of the liturgy of Holy Week has already pointed towards reform of the Mass in the sense suggested, cf. the remarks of Johannes Wagner, director of the Liturgical Institute at Trier: "It has always been the desire of those working for a true renewal of the

Our second example is the Breviary for
secular priests. The conciliar framework of legislation, concentrating once again chiefly on *what*

liturgy that it should, in its whole action, become meaningful again; a meaningful interplay, or, better, combined action and interaction of many, where each has
his own non-interchangeable, untransferrable contribution to make, his own part to play. The new order of
Holy Week shows many tendencies in this direction.
Reading becomes reading once more; only the reader
does it, and the others listen. The singing of the choir
and the singing of the people become themselves again,
and the celebrant does not have to recite their texts
himself, duplicating them, just as though what lector
and choir and people, each in their own role, ritually
perform, were not *dignum et justum*, meet and just.
There are also tendencies suggesting that those who
drew up the new Ordo had their doubts about the
excessive accumulation of introductory and concluding
rites that we now have in the holy Mass. There is also
a very slight indication that perhaps the fundamental
difference between the Service of the Word and the
actual eucharistic celebration is going to be made clearly
visible again in terms of the place where they are performed, and that the altar is going to be reserved for
the celebration of the Eucharist. These are, of course,
only 'tendencies'. The new Ordo is by no means a
unitary work, and there are other elements in it which
contradict these tendencies and the hopes to which
they give rise. Dare we hope that long-cherished expectations are not going to be disappointed, but fulfilled
at last in the near future? Then this renewal of the
Easter Vigil would indeed be the beginning of the great
renewal of the liturgy which the Church needs. God
grant it!" (Postscript to *Paschatis Sollemnia. Studien
zur Osterfeier und Osterfrömmigkeit. Festschrift J. A.
Jungmann, S.J.*, Basle-Freiburg-Vienna, 1959.)

is to be done, could require that the priest should devote a certain space of time in each day (e.g., a total of one hour) to prayer: of which one-third should be mental prayer (to be performed in every possible variety of ways), one-third Scripture reading (with the obligation to work through the entire Bible from Genesis to the Apocalypse, either in one's own language or, for those who wish, in the original languages) and one-third prayer out of the Breviary; this Breviary would be a prayer-book, divided into days, designed for secular priests, consisting of psalms and other prayers.

The episcopate could then work out such a prayer-book for secular priests (i.e., not an adaptation of monastic prayer), with the help of a committee of experts. It could contain psalms, prayers of the Church, ancient and modern, prayers of the great saints and masters of the spiritual life, etc., specially arranged for mornings and evenings and for definite occasions, varying with the Church's year. This priest's prayer-book would then have to be approved by the Pope.

A prayer-book of this sort, in the great, centuries-old tradition of Christian prayer and at the same time appropriate to our times (taking account of the various demands and numerous pressures imposed on our clergy today), could be of immeasurable significance for the spiritual

life of the clergy, combined with the constantly-
repeated reading of the whole text of Holy
Scripture and with mental prayer. The obligation (which, because of human weakness, can
scarcely be dispensed with) would no longer be
to a certain quantity of matter to be recited, but
to a certain amount of *time* to be occupied with
prayer; this would make it easier to avoid the
"vain repetitions" of the heathen (Matt. 6.7)
and, in the midst of our speed-dominated age,
would encourage prayer to be calm, thoughtful,
recollected and serene. The idea is not in the
least to save time but to provide a better form
of prayer. At the same time knowledge and
respect for the Scriptures in their entirety would
be greatly intensified and would exercise an
extremely fertilizing effect on preaching, instruction, pastoral work and theology. In this
way, too, a valuable contribution would be made
not only to renewal within the Church but to
the work of reunion.[1]

[1] On the history of the Breviary, see J. Pascher, article
"Brevier" in the *Lexikon für Theologie und Kirche*,
Freiburg im Breisgau, 1958, 2, 679–84, and the refer-
ences there given (especially to the works of J. Pascher
and J. A. Jungmann). On current hopes (in addition to
the references given in connection with the Mass):
"Brevierstudien. Referate aus der Studientagung von
Assisi 14–17 Sept. 1956", published in the *Auftrag des
Liturgischen Instituts in Trier* by J. A. Jungmann,
Trier, 1958. Here again we must not overlook the far
greater possibilities offered by an ecumenical council.

We could give, as further examples, the administration of the various sacraments, especially baptism, penance and marriage. Here there are already individual examples of rituals, worked out by a national episcopate with the help of experts, and approved by Rome, which represent a good beginning of reform in the sense suggested. All that has been said of the advantages of a reform of the Mass applies, analogously, to the rest of the liturgy.

Finally, and of special importance for reunion, dispensation from the obligation of celibacy (which is purely a matter of ecclesiastical law, and applies only to the Latin Church) for the ordination to the priesthood of married Protestant pastors (already done, in individual cases, by Pius XII), is a matter of the greatest importance. It might also be possible, even in the Latin Church, to find a solution which would be both legally and humanly tolerable (perhaps with an easing of the process of laicizing) for exceptionally hard cases of persistent conflict caused by celibacy. Again, it would be possible to consider the abolition of the obligation of celibacy for deacons. There has for long been a call for married deacons to supplement our heavily overburdened priests; there are numerous reasons in favour of restoring the custom of the early Church, and ceasing to regard the diaconate simply as a preliminary stage to the priesthood. We should also consider a restoration, appropriate to the times, of the Minor Orders.[1]

(b) Under the heading of the bishop's pastoral office, reform of the law of marriage.

Conciliar legislation could decentralize the judging of matrimonial cases, so as to avoid the intolerable delays, often running into many years, which have been prevalent in the past. The bishop's court (or, in the case of very small dioceses, that of the metropolitan) would be the court of first instance, with a second, and final, court of appeal for the country or continent. Thus, for the sake of simplification, and to save time and money, the national or continental episcopate would be competent to set up a central court with highly qualified judges, as indeed already exists in the case of the Spanish Rota, which is a final court of appeal, and a similar court in Germany. Decentralization on these lines could be accompanied by a simplification of matrimonial law and a reduction of unnecessary bureaucracy; e.g., impediments for which the seeking of a dispensation is a pure formality could be abolished altogether. It might also be considered whether, in mixed Catholic-Protestant countries, for the sake of creating a better interconfessional atmosphere, we could

[1] Cf. the symposium, with a wide range of references, edited by P. Winninger, *Vers un renouveau du diaconat*, Paris, 1958 (especially the contributions of J. Hornef, W. Schamoni, J. Loew, F. Arnold, K. Brockmöller, K. Rahner, J. Hofinger, Y. Congar).

not return to the rules for mixed marriages which were in force up to 1918.

The reform of ecclesiastical administration: There would be an enormous easing of pressure if only the principle of subsidiarity were carried to its furthest possible limits in simplification and decentralization. The Council could legislate to transfer quinquennial powers etc. to the bishops as ordinary holders of them (without having to decide the controversy between canonists on the origin of these powers and who held them in the first place). A reduction of the need for dispensations and of ecclesiastical penalties to the absolute minimum (as part of a general reform of the Church's penal rights, which is urgently necessary) would certainly be welcome on all sides (e.g., abolition of those excommunications, for instance in connection with the Index, which are widely regarded as excessive and consequently not regarded at all). One way of balancing administrative decentralization would be to have, as has long and frequently been desired, a stronger representation of local Churches in the Roman Curia, with opportunities for consultation.

Secondly, it would be possible to do something, through general directives, to counteract the natural tendency, latent in every administrative body, to make itself absolute; even administrative bodies (even the Roman Congregations,

which, as we know, do not even have the right to
give authentic interpretations of the *Codex Juris
Canonici*) are plainly, after all, *under* the law.
But it would help if the juridical distinction
between the administrative and the judicial
powers were expressed more clearly in practice,
as would be done if administrative acts were
made subject to judicial investigation.

(c) Under the heading of the bishop's teaching office: The Council could lay the foundation
for a reorganization of book censorship. Intervention should be restricted to really serious
cases, and then it should come from the proper
ecclesiastical authority in the area concerned.
Thus the appropriate procedure would be
graded according to the extent of the damage
being done; the bishop in his diocese (cases are
not likely to occur on this small scale); the
Bishops' Conference (or an episcopal commission) in a country (or continent); Rome only as
a last resort, when the trouble is international.
The author (who is often using all his endeav-
ours, with the best will in the world, on behalf
of the Church) should be protected by a proper
regard for the maintenance of general principles
of law as they apply in any equitable disciplinary
proceeding. If difficulties arise or denunciations
are made, the complaints should be communi-
cated to the author himself, so that he can be
heard and given the opportunity either to defend
or to correct himself; no-one should be con-

demned without the grounds of condemnation being stated; and if a higher authority does have to intervene, it should rely on the lower one for information on the case.

A thorough reform (or even abolition) of the Index should be considered. Even at Rome the view is taken that the Index no longer fulfils its purpose (it is largely unknown, it is no longer understood, and it is not taken seriously; it includes reputable Catholic theologians, on account of minor aberrations, in the same list as atheists, pornographers, etc.); indeed, it tends to have the opposite effect to that intended, ensuring to any book placed upon it the widest possible circulation. Nowadays, when the only authority recognized in spiritual matters is a moral one, a *warning* about a book, with solid grounds given for it, would be more effective than a prohibition against reading it without any statement of the reasons. Indeed, it would often be the case—again in accordance with the principle of subsidiarity (see the quotation from Father Bertrams on p. 239)—that to allow free discussion would do more to clarify a problem and to set men's minds at rest than any hasty condemnation.[1]

[1] Cf. an article written, with reference to the coming Council, under the pseudonym of "Felix Lektor", "Der Index der verbotenen Bücher", in *Orientierung*, 23 (1959), 124–9 (with some valuable references to proposals made by the French and German episcopates at the Vatican Council).

Under the heading of the teaching office we can also, of course, think of positive things to be done: for instance, the raising of the standard of preaching and theological study. A great contribution would be made to a better preparation for the preaching ministry and to a deeper theological formation if scriptural theology were developed still further throughout the Church, and especially in seminaries.

In this connection, there is something of great importance that needs to be pointed out: few things could perhaps be so beneficial to the inner renewal of the Church (and so, indirectly, to the cause of reunion) as a manifestation, on the part of the Council, of the redemptive significance of the Word of God. It was not for nothing that, even at the Vatican Council, the Holy Scriptures, lying upon a throne in full view of all the bishops, formed, together with the altar, the focal point of the Church there assembled. A solemn confession of faith by the Council in the Word of God, a confession that would leave aside controversies over the exact relation of Scripture to tradition while continuing the positive line of development running through Trent and the Vatican, proclaiming the pre-eminent significance of the Word of God over every word of man, proclaiming its power to pardon, to save, to illuminate, to strengthen, to console—such a declaration could have an

extraordinarily beneficial effect on every area of
the Church's life: liturgy, preaching, catechesis,
theology, pastoral work and the spiritual life.

Such are our examples of practical ways of
restoring its full value to the episcopal office.
But there is an objection, not to be ignored,
which will no doubt be made against them. We
do not mean so much the difficulty that the
uneven quality, in practice, of the episcopate in
various countries gives little hope that such
powers, when given, will always be well and
appropriately used. Obviously, every regime has
its own characteristic dangers; but a good legislative framework, good inter-connecting links
between the various episcopates and their expert
advisers, and finally good supervision and effective control from Rome can reduce these dangers to a manageable minimum. But there is
another, more important objection: Would not
decentralization on these lines lead to a new
centralization in the bishop, with consequences
as undesirable on a small scale as those of Roman
centralism on a large scale? Are not we in the
Church often glad that we can appeal to Rome?
Such appeals would of course remain possible
in the new regime as well. And no doubt the
bishops themselves will see the dangers. Further,
the possibilities that we have indicated envisage
an increase in the effective authority not primarily of the individual bishop but of the local

episcopate. But, setting this aside, it will also (again in accordance with the principle of subsidiarity) be the by no means easy task of the bishop to continue the work of decentralization, delegating as much power downwards as he can and working especially for a close and personal relationship between bishop and clergy, and between bishop and people. According to the ancient doctrine, the Church is in the bishop, but the bishop is not the Church; as the bishops are the *pleroma* of the Church, so the people are the *pleroma* of the bishop.

We should consider at this point that to avoid giving a false, authoritarian, clericalist impression of the Church by defining the rights of bishops, and to complete the formulation of the doctrine of the Church begun at the Vatican Council, a *declaration of principle* on the significance of the *layman* in the Church would be very welcome (and certainly in accord with the expectations of our time). The time does not yet seem ripe for a revision of Canon Law on the subject of the laity; it could certainly, and obviously, not be done by a codification of the various forms of "Catholic Action", differing strongly as they do from one country to another; anything of the sort would be as likely to check positive developments as to encourage them. But a declaration of principle could, in an age which is for many reasons being called an "Age of the

Laity", be of the greatest theological and practical significance for the Church. Here again
there are of course many theological questions
that are still unclear,[1] but it must be possible
to give clear and illuminating expression to the
fundamental truth. The scriptural concept of
the Body of Christ, of which *all* Christians are
members, and of the royal priesthood, to which
all Christians are called by baptism, would form
the solid foundation for a specific theological
declaration that the layman does not belong to
the Church in some secondary sense but that he
is the Church, not only as a passive, receptive
object to be cared for, but as an active subject,
taking the initiative, and co-responsible for the
Church.[2] This would be the starting-point for
a brief outline of the liturgical, canonical and

[1] Among new works on the theology of the laity, cf.
Y. Congar, O.P., *Lay People in the Church*, London,
1957; F. X. Arnold, *Kirche und Laientum*, Tübingen,
1954; H. U. von Balthasar, *Der Laie und die Kirche*,
Einsiedeln, 1954; G. Philips, *Le Rôle du laïcat dans
l'Eglise*, Tournai, 1954; K. Rahner "Über das Laien-
apostolat", in *Schriften zur Theologie*, Einsiedeln, 1955,
2, 339–73; A. Sustar, "Der Laie in der Kirche", in
Fragen der Theologie heute, ed. Feiner, Trütsch and
Böckle, Einsiedeln, 1957, 519–48; H. Küng, *Ehr seid
eine königliche Priesterschaft. Faszikel 2 der Arbeits-
mappe für die Frauen- und Mütterseelsorge*, Lucerne,
1958.

[2] Cf. Pius XII's address to the newly-appointed cardinals in 1946, and to the Second World Congress of
the Lay Apostolate in 1957.

apostolic function of the layman in the Church
and his position in the world (his performance
of a "divine office" in and for the world, in the
family, in his profession, and in social life); the
justification of a distinct, characteristic lay
spirituality; and the relationship of the laity to
the Hierarchy. To show that the Church's
leaders really mean these declarations, it would
be an impressive gesture if, not only in the
Eastern rite, but, as would be perfectly possible,
in the Latin rite too, the chalice were, in principle, restored to the laity.

Finally, let us suggest two last possibilities
which, if put into action, would make the whole
world listen. The Council could speak a word
of repentance, and it could speak a word of faith.

A word of repentance: we in the Church are
none of us guiltless of the world's unhappy state
today, and the guilt of our fathers lies heavy
upon us too. It would be a truly Christian act if
the Pope and the Council (perhaps at the very
beginning, when they are invoking the Holy
Spirit) were to express this truth: Forgive us our
sins! Forgive us our sins, and in particular our
share in the sin of schism! Pope Adrian VI said
it, long ago. An honest, humble confession of
this sort by the leaders of the Church today
would be pleasing to our heavenly Father as few
words or deeds could be; and one word of repentance would open more doors to us amongst our

separated fellow-Christians than any number of pressing invitations to return.

A word of faith: the troubled and fearful world of today may surely hope to receive from an ecumenical council some word of power, of consolation, of confidence; not only "decrees" on doctrine and discipline but, as from the early councils, a *confession of faith*; a joyful and courageous confession of faith in the living God, who is as near to us as ever in this age of artificial satellites and space-travel, who has not forgotten us in the sufferings of two World Wars and the menace of atomic death, but who is merciful to us in his Son Jesus Christ, upon whose coming we wait in confidence, that God may be all in all.

These, then, are certain possibilities for a council in our time, as they take shape against the background of the theological and historical analysis we have made here. It seems to us that the fulfilment of these possibilities would tend towards that which we may hope from the Council: a restoration of the office of the bishop, and of the local Church which he embodies, both at the level of dogmatic theory and at that of practical organization; and through this, a radical, interior renewal of the life of the Church: all as a necessary preparation for ultimate reunion.

These possibilities that we have indicated do

not attack anything that is inviolable in Catholicism nor surrender anything that is essential. No doubt they will seem bold to many, perhaps overbold to some. But all the preceding chapters should have shown that it is *bold* measures that are needed today. Is it illusory to think of such possibilities? We must answer with a counter-question: Is it not illusory *not* to think of such possibilities, to have an illusory notion of what are, in the concrete, the conditions necessary for renewal and reunion?

3. REUNION BY DEGREES

Even if these possibilities do become realities (and we should most earnestly hope that it is the next Council rather than the next but one that puts them into operation), this would still not mean the attainment of reunion. Four hundred, nay, a thousand years of separated Churches cannot be crossed at a single bound. It will need step after step. But let it be by all means an energetic, generous striding-out and not a vague, petty feeling our way.

And do not say that even if we Catholics did all this, the Protestants still would not change. No denomination lives in a world of its own. If *we* change, the others cannot help changing too. So do not say that even if we do all this to let the light of the Petrine office shine more clearly, the Protestants would still never accept any Petrine office in the modern Church. No, let us first do what is *ours* to do—and then the others will no longer be what they are today. Many a one who is still protesting loudly against this or that today will only be protesting quietly to-morrow—and the day after tomorrow, perhaps not at all, for he will have realized that in the meanwhile his protest has lost its object. So let *us*, here and now, take one large, bold, well-planned stride—and not worry whether or not reunion will follow hard upon it. Sufficient unto the day is the evil thereof—and are we Christians, then, abandoned by the good God?

Besides this, the great point of the possibilities suggested above is that their value is not restricted to their effect on outsiders. True, we should expect to find that if they were put into practice they would be thankfully recognized as a great step forward both by Protestants and (indeed primarily) by the Orthodox (while we have been speaking almost entirely of Protestant demands, the demands of the Orthodox are in many respects the same). But the best thing about these possibilities is that carrying them out would mean a purer and fuller realization of Catholicism itself: a fundamental renewal of the Catholic Church. Even if the reaction of our separated brethren were disappointing, this would not detract from the Christian value of

these possibilities. The primary consideration
is not whether we shall stand better in the eyes
of Protestants or Orthodox, but whether we shall
stand better in the eyes of our Lord Jesus Christ.
For him, and for the glory of the Father, and for
the coming of his Kingdom, we must do our
best in the Church—and all the rest shall be
added unto us.

The task before the Council is gigantic. For
this reason we may hope that it will not meet
too soon. Only a supremely well-prepared Council can be a successful Council. Good preparation means preparation on a generous scale. Not
one of the reforming decrees of the Vatican
Council reached the point of adoption, because
they were all too petty. We Catholics may in
this matter take to heart the hopes of the famous
Orthodox theologian George Florowsky:

> There is unquestionably at this time a
> flowering of theology and liturgy going on in
> the Roman Church. But the new movement,
> symptom and pledge of a vital creative
> activity, has not yet affected anything like the
> whole Church, nor has it penetrated her at
> every level. The preparations for the Council
> are, it seems, to be theologically unimpas-
> sioned and "non-party"; which could not, un-
> fortunately, be said of the preparations for the
> Vatican Council. It is to be hoped that the

preliminary work for the Council will be conducted at the level of theological thought which has been achieved at this time within the Roman Church. The manifold variety and the whole scope of this thought, and spiritual experiences both within and without the Roman Church, should be taken into account in this preliminary work, with wise and sensitive discretion . . . It is especially to be hoped that the preparatory work for the Council will show sufficient awareness of achievements within the Roman Church in modern biblical scholarship and ecclesiastical history. The Council must not be deficient either in its exegesis or in its understanding of the Church's history. We may hope that in its dogmatic debates more scope will be given to the witness of the Fathers of the Church than has been the case since the beginning of the scholastic period.[1]

It is indeed especially important during the time of preparation to listen to the voice of non-Catholic communions: Orthodox, Anglican and Protestant. We Catholics cannot, in this connection, overlook the fact that almost all non-Catholic Christian communions are included in the World Council of Churches. We cannot

[1] G. Florowsky, "Das bevorstehende Konzil der römischen Kirche", in *Una Sancta*, 14 (1959), 173 f.

overlook the fact that in the World Council, in spite of all the differences in principle that there are, a great work has already been done for unity. This work has not been done *against* us but—understood aright—*for* us. We also realize that a reunion with the Orthodox to the detriment of the Protestants would be pointless. But surely those on the Protestant side will understand if the Catholic Church does perhaps concentrate her efforts rather on the side where reunion is more readily possible.

The Pope himself has spoken of an approach to reunion by degrees: approach (*avvicinamento*), then coming together (*riaccostamento*), and finally perfect unity (*unità perfetta*).[1] There are two things to be noted here.

The "approach" takes place on the basis of what we hold strongly in common. Our separated brethren are already brethren. There is already a deep communion, *koinonia*, between them and us; it is founded on one baptism, faith in one Lord, and love for him; and it is stronger and more important than anything that separates us. *We* are Christians, and *they are Christians;* "They too bear the name of Christ upon their foreheads, they read his holy and blessed Gospel, and they are not unreceptive to the stirrings of religious devotion and of active, beneficent love

[1] John XXIII, Letter to the Venetian Clergy, 24 April 1959. (*Herder-Korrespondenz* (1959–60), p. 413.)

of their neighbour."[1] What we need for reunion is that this communion which already exists should *grow*. What we need is that both sides should create more and more common ground between us, until at last what separates us becomes insignificant and full unity is a reality.

This "perfect unity" will not be uniformity. As the Pope has said, it will be unity in essentials, freedom in all else. It is quite unthinkable that after centuries of separation we could be reduced not only to a common denominator but to a single numerator. What we can have is unity in the sense of the living *koinonia* of the Scriptures, which is unity in *diversity*, unity in a variety of rites, languages, customs, modes of thought and action and prayer. Such unity is more perfect than uniformity.

Will there be reunion? We base nothing upon our own strength; our unshakable hope is in the Holy Spirit:

SEND FORTH THY SPIRIT
AND THOU SHALT RENEW THE FACE OF THE EARTH!

[1] John XXIII, Christmas Message 1958, *Herder-Korrespondenz* (1959–60), p. 241.

APPENDICES

APPENDIX 1

A DECLARATION BY THE GERMAN BISHOPS ON THE RELATION BETWEEN THE EPISCOPATE AND THE PAPAL PRIMACY

As we have said already, the meaning of the episcopal office is being brought into the foreground by the coming Council. For this reason we are giving here an extremely important declaration of principle by the German bishops after the Vatican Council (1875) on the status of bishops in the Catholic Church. This declaration was not only taken up by the English episcopate and by Cardinal Dechamps of Mechlin, but was also solemnly approved by Pius IX himself in a brief to the German bishops on 2 March 1875: ". . . Your declaration is an expression of that true Catholic doctrine which is at once the teaching of the Vatican Council and of the Holy See" (and again in his consistorial address of 15 March 1875).

We are giving this declaration, which was published in *Der Katholik* no. 55 (1875), pp. 209–13, together with a commentary by Dom Olivier Rousseau, O.S.B., of Chevetogne, taken, by kind permission of the editors, from the bulletin for inter-confessional contacts, *Una Sancta*, no. 12 (1957), pp. 226–8. This document is offered here not for its political but for its theological bearing, and hence the reader should not let himself be distracted by references to the current political situation at that time.

COLLECTIVE DECLARATION BY THE GERMAN EPISCOPATE ON THE CIRCULAR OF THE IMPERIAL GERMAN CHANCELLOR CONCERNING THE NEXT PAPAL ELECTION

The *Staats-Anzeiger* recently published a circular from the Chancellor, Prince Bismarck, of 14 May 1872, on the subject of the next papal election, which, so the *Anzeiger* expressly states, formed the whole basis of that part of the documents relating to Church-State relations which was withheld from the public at the trial of Graf von Armin.

The circular starts from the presupposition that "the Vatican Council and its two most important decisions on the infallibility and jurisdiction of the Pope have completely altered the position of the latter in relation to government", and hence that "governmental interest in the papal election is increased in the highest degree, now that the Government's right to be concerned about it has been given a much firmer foundation."

These conclusions are as unjustified as the presupposition on which they are based is itself unfounded; and considering the importance of the document, and the conclusion drawn from it by those responsible in the Chancery for the affairs of the Church in Germany, the under-signed pastors feel it to be both their right and their duty, in the interests of truth, to make a public declaration against the views contained in it.

The circular asserts, in regard to the decisions of the Vatican Council: "Through these deci-sions the Pope has reached the position of taking the rights of the bishops in every single diocese into his own hands and substituting the papal authority for that of the national episcopate." "Episcopal jurisdiction has been absorbed into papal." "The Pope no longer, as hitherto, exer-cises certain definite reserved rights, but holds the whole of the bishops' rights in his hands." "He has in principle taken the place of each individual bishop", ". . . and it rests entirely with him whether he will, in practice, at any given moment, take the place of the bishop in relation to the Government." "The bishops are now no more than his tools, his officials, without responsibility of their own." "In relation to the Government, they have become the officials of a foreign sovereign", ". . . and, furthermore, of a sovereign whose infallibility makes him totally

10*

absolute, beyond any absolute monarch in the world."

Each of these statements is without foundation, and is in flat contradiction to the decisions of the Vatican Council, both in their wording and in the true sense in which they have been repeatedly explained by the Pope, the bishops, and Catholic scholars.

According to these decisions, the ecclesiastical jurisdictional authority of the Pope is indeed a "potestas suprema, ordinaria et immediata", a supreme authority, conferred upon the Pope in the person of St. Peter by Jesus Christ the Son of God, extending over the whole Church, and so over each diocese and directly over all the faithful, for the preservation of unity of faith, of discipline and of the government of the Church, and certainly not merely consisting of a few reserved rights.

But this is not a new doctrine; it is a truth of the Catholic faith which has always been recognized, and a well-known principle of canon law, a doctrine which the Vatican Council has declared and affirmed afresh against the errors of the Gallicans, Jansenists and Febronians and in union with the pronouncements of earlier general councils. According to this doctrine of the Catholic Church the Pope is Bishop of Rome, not bishop of any other city or diocese, not Bishop of Cologne or Breslau or anywhere else. But as Bishop of Rome he is, at the same time, Pope, i.e., shepherd and head of the whole Church, head of all the bishops and all the faithful, and his papal authority does not simply come to life in certain exceptional cases but has power and validity always and everywhere. Being in this position, the Pope has to see to it that each bishop carries out the whole of the duties of his office, and where a bishop is prevented from doing so, or any other necessity demands it, the Pope has the right and duty, not as bishop of the diocese in question but as Pope, to order everything in it which appertains to its administration. All the states of Europe have, until this present time, recognized these papal rights as belonging to the system of the Catholic Church, and in their dealings with the Papal See they have always regarded the occupant of it as the real head of the whole Catholic Church, of the bishops as well as of the faithful, and by no means simply as the holder of certain reserved rights.

Nor do the decisions of the Vatican Council give any shadow of ground for stating that they have made the Pope an absolute sovereign, more totally absolute, by virtue of his infallibility, than any absolute monarch in the world.

In the first place, the field in which the Pope's ecclesiastical authority operates is essentially different from that in which the secular sovereignty of a monarch operates; nor is the full sovereignty of the ruling prince, in the affairs of the State, disputed by Catholics. But quite apart from this, the description of absolute monarch, even with reference to the Church's affairs, cannot be applied to the Pope, because he stands under the divine law and is bound by the provisions made by Christ for his Church. He cannot change the constitution given to the Church by her divine founder, as a secular legislator can alter the constitution of a state. The constitution of the Church rests in all essential points on divine ordinances and is exempt from all human arbitration. It is in virtue of the same divine institution upon which the Papacy rests that the episcopate also exists; it, too, has its rights and its duties, because of the ordinance of God himself, and the Pope has neither the right nor the power to change them. Thus it is a complete misunderstanding of the Vatican decisions to believe that because of them "episcopal jurisdiction has been absorbed into papal", that the Pope has "in principle taken the place of each individual bishop", that the bishops are now "no more than tools of the Pope, his officials, without responsibility of their own". According to the constant teaching of the Catholic Church, expressly declared at the Vatican Council itself, the bishops are not mere tools of the Pope, nor papal officials without responsibility of their own, but "appointed by the Holy Spirit and occupying the place of the Apostles, they nourish and rule, as true shepherds, the flocks committed to their charge."

As throughout the last eighteen hundred years of Christian history the Primacy, with and over the episcopate which is like itself ordained by Christ, has by virtue of its divine appointment continued as a part of the organism of the Church and worked for her well-being, so it will continue. And as the rights of the Pope, which have always existed, to exercise his ecclesiastical authority throughout the Catholic world, have not hitherto tended to make the authority of the bishops illusory, neither can this new declaration of the old Catholic doctrine of the Primacy give any grounds for such a fear for the future. It is indeed common knowledge that the dioceses of the whole Catholic world have continued to be governed by their bishops since the Vatican Council in exactly the same way as before.

As for the assertion that the decisions of the Vatican Council have made the bishops into papal officials without responsibility of their own, we can only reject it with all possible emphasis; it is, indeed, not in the Catholic Church that the immoral and despotic principle that the command of a superior releases one from responsibility has found acceptance.

Finally, the view that the Pope is in virtue of his infallibility "a totally absolute sovereign" rests on a completely erroneous notion of the dogma of papal infallibility. As the Vatican Council expressed it in clear, precise words, and as proceeds from the very nature of the case, infallibility refers simply to the character of the supreme papal teaching authority; this covers precisely the same field as the infallible teaching office of the Church in general, and is limited to what is contained in the Scriptures and Tradition and the doctrinal decisions already made by the Church's teaching office.

The governmental dealings of the Pope are not affected by it to the very slightest degree. If it is once realized that the opinion that the relation of the Pope to the episcopate has been changed by the Vatican decisions is completely groundless, then the conclusion drawn from this, that the Pope's relation to governments has been changed by them, loses any possible basis as well.

We cannot, moreover, refrain from expressing our deep concern that the Chancellor should, in this circular, have based his judgement of Catholic affairs upon assertions and hypotheses which have been put into circulation by certain former Catholics who have gone to the length of openly attacking the legitimate authority of the episcopate and of the Holy See, and by a number of Protestant scholars, but which have been repeatedly and emphatically rejected and denied by the Pope, the bishops, and Catholic theologians and canonists.

As the lawful representatives of the Catholic Church in the dioceses entrusted to our leadership, we have the right to demand that when the principles and doctrines of our Church are to be judged, we should be heard; and so long as we conduct ourselves according to these principles and doctrines, we surely may expect that men will accord us belief.

While correcting, in this present declaration, the version of Catholic doctrine contained in the Chancellor's circular, it is not our intention to go any further into what is said in the circular on the subject of the next papal election.

We feel obliged, however, to raise our voices in loud and solemn protest against the attack there attempted against the full freedom and independence of the Catholic Church to choose her supreme head; at the same time we shall point out that it is only the authority of the Church which can at any time pronounce on the validity of a papal election, and to that decision every Catholic, in Germany as in every other country, will submit without reservation.

[Then follow the signatures of the twenty-three prelates forming the Catholic hierarchy of Germany.]

Commentary by Dom Olivier Rousseau, O.S.B.

It must be observed that in Bismarck's circular—leaving aside everything aimed at involving the question with politics—all the seven points made are concerned with the authority of the bishops and their supposed absorption into the papal jurisdiction since the Vatican Council. This is the kernel of the whole argument, and the reason for the vigorous response of the bishops and of Pius IX. It concerns, in fact, a dogmatically very important element in the Church's structure. Even though, in practice, the Council's clarification of the juridical position was limited to the prerogatives of the Bishop of Rome, yet it is obvious that the decisions of the Council did not, in this matter, go beyond the definition of a doctrine which had long been held in the Church, and that they changed absolutely nothing, most particularly nothing in respect of the episcopate. Each single one of the seven assertions in the circular must be regarded as "in flat contradiction" to the decisions of the Council and to Catholic teaching. Hence, in order to express this teaching we need do no more than affirm the opposite of each of these assertions:

(1) The Pope *cannot* lay claim to the rights of the bishops or substitute his authority for theirs.

(2) Episcopal jurisdiction *is not* absorbed into papal jurisdiction.

(3) The decisions of the Vatican Council *did not* place the whole of episcopal authority in the hands of the Pope.

(4) He *has not* in principle taken the place of each individual bishop.

(5) He *cannot*, in relations with the Government, put himself in the bishop's place at any given moment.

(6) The bishops *have not* become tools of the Pope.

(7) They *are not*, in their relations with the Government, officials of a foreign sovereign.

"Each of these statements", the bishops emphasize—meaning each of Bismarck's assertions—"is without foundation, and is in flat contradiction to the decisions of the Vatican Council, both in their wording and in their true sense." The Pope is and remains Bishop of Rome, and he is neither Bishop of Cologne nor of Breslau nor anywhere else. He is Pope as being Bishop of Rome, and successor to St. Peter in the apostolic see of that Church. The Pope is under the divine law and is bound by Christ's ordinances for his Church. Hence he cannot alter the constitution given to the Church by her divine founder. The episcopate was set up by that same divine founder, just as much as the Papacy. The Pope has neither the right nor the power to alter anything in this. The bishops are not papal officials, but "appointed by the Holy Spirit and occupying the place of the Apostles, they nourish and rule, as true shepherds, the flocks committed to their charge".

And Pius IX praised the German bishops because they had in this fashion declared "the true meaning of the Vatican decrees" and had thus prevented the faithful from "forming a false idea of them".

He recognized that this declaration of the bishops is so exact that "it leaves nothing to be desired"; to such an extent "that it is not necessary for the Pope to add anything to it". He wishes solemnly to reaffirm it himself simply for the sake of those who thought they saw in it an attempt to explain away the Council, in a sense contrary to the intentions of the Holy See. The bishops' declaration is "true Catholic doctrine", "clearly and irrefutably demonstrated and . . . precisely expressed".

The direct and brusque character of these declarations by the bishops and the Pope, due to their spontaneous and indignant reaction, lends its full and total support to the clearest of dogmatic truths concerning the episcopate. On this ground alone, Bismarck's accusations may be regarded as providential. For it is the peculiarity of these documents that they (unlike the texts generally used on this subject, which treat of the episcopate and the Papacy together) represent the testimony of the teaching office on the subject of the episcopate *alone*; which is easy to understand, since all the rest had been said at the Council.

The factual content on which all this is based is indeed strictly limited and concentrated: the bishops are appointed by Christ, who ordained the twelve Apostles whose successors they are; thus it will remain until the end of time, and nothing can be changed in this essential structure of the Church.

APPENDIX 2

CHRONOLOGICAL TABLE OF THE TWENTY ECUMENICAL COUNCILS SO FAR HELD IN THE HISTORY OF THE CHURCH

This table is taken from Hubert Jedin's *Ecumenical Councils of the Catholic Church* (London and Edinburgh, Nelson, 1960), which provides an admirable historical complement to this book.

(1) First Council of Nicaea, 20 May to 25[?] July, 325. Pope Sylvester I, 314–35. Nicene Creed against Arius; the Son consubstantial with the Father. Twenty canons.

(2) First Council of Constantinople, May to July 381. Pope Damasus 1, 366–84. Nicene-Constantinopolitan Creed: the divinity of the Holy Ghost. Four canons.

(3) Council of Ephesus. Five sessions, 22 June to 17 July, 431. Pope Celestine I, 422–32. Mary, the Mother of God, against Nestorius. Six canons.

(4) Council of Chalcedon. Seventeen sessions, 8 Oct. to 1 Nov. 451. Pope Leo I, the Great, 440–61. Two natures in the one person of Christ. Twenty-eight canons.

(5) Second Council of Constantinople. Eight sessions, 5 May to 2 June, 553. Pope Vigilius, 537–55. Condemnation of the "Three Chapters" of the Nestorians.

(6) Third Council of Constantinople. Sixteen sessions, 7 Nov. 680 to 16 Sept. 681 (*in Trullo*). Pope Agatho, 678–81; Pope Leo II, 682–3. Condemnation of the doctrine of one will in Christ (Monotheletism); Question of Honorius.

(7) Second Council of Nicaea. Eight sessions, 24 Sept. to 23 Oct. 787. Pope Hadrian I, 772–95. Meaning and lawfulness of the veneration of images. Twenty canons.

(8) Fourth Council of Constantinople. Ten sessions, 5 Oct. 869 to 28 Feb. 870. Pope Nicholas I, 858–67; Hadrian II, 867–72. Termination of the schism of Patriarch Photius. Twenty-seven canons.

(9) First Lateran Council, 18 March to 6 April 1123. Pope Callistus II, 1119–24. Confirmation of the Concordat of Worms. Twenty-five canons.

(10) Second Lateran Council, April 1139. Pope Innocent II, 1130–43. Schism of Anacletus II. Thirty canons.

(11) Third Lateran Council. Three sessions, 5 to 19 (or 22) March 1179. Pope Alexander III, 1159–81. Twenty-seven chapters; two-thirds majority for papal election.

(12) Fourth Lateran Council. Three sessions, 11 to 30 Nov. 1215. Pope Innocent III, 1198–1216. Seventy chapters: Profession of faith against the Cathari; change of substance in the Eucharist; annual confession and Communion.

(13) First Council of Lyons. Three sessions, 28 June to 17 July 1245. Pope Innocent IV, 1243–54. Deposition of the Emperor Frederick II. Twenty-two chapters.

(14) Second Council of Lyons. Six sessions, 7 May to 17 July 1274. Pope Gregory X, 1271–6. Rules for Conclave, union with the Greeks, Crusade. Thirty-one chapters.

(15) Council of Vienne. Three sessions, 16 Oct. 1311 to 6 May 1312. Pope Clement V, 1305–14. Suppression of the Order of the Templars. Controversy over Franciscan poverty. Reform decrees.

(16) Council of Constance. Forty-five sessions, 5 Nov. 1414 to 22 April 1418. Termination of the Great Schism; resignation of the Roman Pope Gregory XII (1405–15) on 4 July 1415; deposition of the conciliar Pope John XXIII (1410–15) on 29 May 1415; deposition of the Avignon Pope, Benedict XIII (1394–1415) on 26 July 1417. Election of Martin V, 11 Nov. 1417. Condemnation of John Hus. Decree *Sacrosancta* on the superiority of the Council over the Pope and decree *Frequens* on the period-

icity of councils. Concordats with five conciliar nations.

(17) Council of Basle-Ferrara-Florence. At Basle
twenty-five sessions, 23 July 1431 to 7 May
1437. Translation to Ferrara by Eugenius
IV (1431–47) on 18 Sept. 1437, finally on
1 Jan. 1438; from there to Florence, 16 Jan.
1439. Union with the Greeks, 6 July 1439,
with the Armenians, 22 Nov. 1439, with the
Jacobites, 4 Feb. 1442. Translation to Rome
25 April 1442.

(18) Fifth Lateran Council. Twelve sessions, 10
May 1512 to 16 March 1517. Pope Julius
II, 1503–13; Leo X, 1513–21. Against the
schismatic Council of Pisa, 1511–12. Reform
decrees.

(19) Council of Trent. Twenty-five sessions, 13
Dec. 1545 to 4 Dec. 1563, in three periods:
sessions 1–8 at Trent 1545–47; sessions 9–11
at Bologna 1547, all under Paul III, 1534–
49; sessions 12–16 again at Trent 1551–52,
under Pope Julius III, 1550–5, sessions
17–25 at Trent under Pius IV, 1559–65.
Doctrine of Scripture and Tradition,
original sin and justification, sacraments
and sacrifice of the Mass, veneration of the
saints, reform decrees.

(20) Council of the Vatican. Four sessions, 8 Dec.
1869 to 18 July 1870. Pope Pius IX, 1846–
78. Definitions of Catholic doctrine, the
Pope's primacy and his infallibility.

INDEX

INDEX